It's Warm in Siberia

It's Warm in
Siberia

TRAVEL STORIES AND PHOTOGRAPHS
FROM A SOLO JOURNEY ACROSS THE USSR IN 1984

Jon Humboldt Gates

SECOND EDITION COPYRIGHT 2023 BY JON HUMBOLDT GATES

All rights reserved. No part of this book may be reproduced in any form or by any electronic or mechanical means without prior written consent of the publisher, except for quotation of brief, attributed passages.

First Edition Copyright ©1988 by Jon Humboldt Gates

PUBLISHER'S NOTE – This book was originally published in 1988 by Summer Run Publishing, Eureka, California, under the title SOVIET PASSAGE. That title was discontinued with all publishing rights reserved by the author. Moonstone Publishing is re-releasing the book as IT'S WARM IN SIBERIA, a second edition, with design, editorial and photographic revisions.

Second edition editor – Katie Sanborn

Cover and book design – Renée Davis

First edition editor – Beverly Hanley

Cover Photo: Siberian Village on the Angara River – by Elenmay – iStockphoto

Published By:

Info@moonstonepublishing.com

P.O. Box 292
Lake Oswego, OR 97034

Printed in the United States
ISBN #978-1-878136-04-6

"I suppose that at first, it was people who invented borders, and then borders started to invent people."

Yevgeny Yevtushenko

Contents

Preface 9

Nakhodka 11

It's Warm in Siberia 17

A Long Way to Perm 59

The Golden Ring 73

Finding Petrodvorets 97

Along the Dneiper 131

Crossing Belarus 147

Yuri, from Kamchatka 153

Seven Years Later 165

Preface

When I first traveled across the USSR, in 1984, the country was showing the first signs of opening after decades of isolation. Its people were eager to engage and hopeful, despite their inability to travel abroad and lack of access to foreign currency. They prized education. Healthcare was a given. Public transportation and housing were relatively inexpensive. I was just 33 years old in 1984, and I embraced their idealism. In the decades since then, I have crisscrossed five continents, including periodic trips back into Ukraine and Russia, got married in Moscow in 1991, and published two new, non-fiction books.

The rapid change unleashed inside Russia after the USSR banners came down was a stunning spectacle: high-rise business centers, massive highway expansions, historic Orthodox churches brought back to life, mega traffic jams, dachas constructed like small palaces, and enormous private enterprise developments. These modernizations recast the character of major cities. More people had money, higher paying jobs, and they could now travel internationally. By 2015, parts of the country became almost unrecognizable from the places I saw in 1984.

This collection of stories and vignettes is but a young traveler's glimpse into the lives of ordinary people during the final years of the USSR, a snapshot of a time in history. Though I have lost touch with many of the people I met during the Soviet era, what remains is the deep sense of personal discovery and mutual curiosity that I experienced while traveling there, dispelling the notions of gray hopelessness and privation that popular media conveyed at the time. I found humor, intellect, joy, creativity, and sorrow among those whom I met. They possessed an enthusiasm to engage. It was not George Orwell's 1984.

It's Warm in Siberia is being released as a second edition to the original book I wrote about my travels, *Soviet Passage*, published in 1988. I have added new stories and additional detail to previous stories. My original USSR travel journals and all of my photos are long gone, destroyed by a wildfire that took down our home in 2017, but as I re-engaged with the stories for this new edition, I found the memories still so vivid, so detailed, so deeply embedded, that I was compelled to expand on my 1984 writings.

On a practical level, I have chosen to leave place names as they were then and not update them, in keeping with the era and my place in it. For example, Leningrad is Leningrad, and not St. Petersburg; Kalinin is referenced, not Tver; and the spelling of Kiev was not altered to reflect the current spelling of Kyiv.

As I worked on this second edition, a great tragedy was unfolding across the frontier of Russia and Ukraine, which could never have been imagined by me, my wife, or any of the people I met there in 1984. Some of the people in this travelogue were from Ukraine, some from Russia, and a few from other Soviet republics. No matter where they were from, the people I met across the USSR in the waning days of the nation were universally hopeful for a better world and a peaceful future for all of us, and they welcomed me, a foreigner in their midst.

I have added an epilogue to this second edition that describes events that followed my first trip into the USSR in 1984. It covers seven more years. During that time, I returned to Kiev and Moscow numerous times, working on a World Beat music collaboration between Soviet and American musicians, called *Timezone*, which resulted in the album, *Lost Nations*. The final recordings of the project were completed in Moscow in December 1991, during the week the Soviet Union collapsed.

jhg

Nakhodka

This trip began long before the 747 lifted off the runway in San Francisco in the summer of 1984, bound for Tokyo, where I would board a ship to the USSR. It might have begun under my school desk in the late 1950s, practicing bomb drills. I was one of the millions of American kids who watched civil defense test patterns on TV. Nikita Khrushchev pounded his shoe on the table at the United Nations, and the Cuban missile crisis mushroomed. Soviet armored divisions paraded with atomic rockets in Red Square. Americans dug bomb shelters.

As kids, we learned to talk about what we wanted to be when we grew up, despite being aware that our future was wired for global destruction.

The Soviet ship *Khabarovsk* was an outpost of the USSR, sailing across the Sea of Japan from Yokohama to the seaport of Nakhodka, north of Vladivostok, broadcasting Russian music and announcements over the ship's public address system and serving Russian food. Images of Konstantin Chernenko, the leader of the Soviet Union, were mounted in the ship's common areas. Cyrillic signs marked the passageways. Red and gold Soviet flags snapped in the breeze. The crew spoke in Russian.

The *Khabarovsk* was a small, coastal passenger freighter, with about one hundred people aboard including the crew. The ship's holds were packed with con-

tainers of freight. Passengers were a mix of Soviet tourists returning from Japan, Japanese tourists on their way to the USSR, a Hungarian Bartok choir on tour, one Polish university student, and me—the only American on board. The ship's steward assigned us to specific dining tables for the duration of the voyage. He didn't know what to do with me, so he put me at a table with five Japanese tourists. A couple of them spoke a little bit of English, and I spoke no Japanese. When they realized I was traveling alone they took great pity on me, as if there'd been a death in the family, and tried to make me feel part of their group.

On the third day at sea, I stood at the bow of the *Khabarovsk* and watched for the coast of the Soviet Far East. An older Japanese man from Hiroshima leaned against the rail alongside me, talking about life in his city after World War II. His expression was solemn, reserved. He had been a child when the first atomic bomb was dropped, on Hiroshima. Having survived, he forever was committed to peace after having witnessed the bombing's horrific outcome. We listened to the hiss of white water and the cry of seagulls as gray ocean mists gave way to a long dark rampart across the western horizon. My first glimpse of the Soviet Far East.

Only a week before, I'd been with my father aboard his commercial fishing boat off the coast of Northern California. I had lived most of my life beside redwood forests, around the seaport of Humboldt Bay, a provincial area balanced between wilderness and industry. By 1984, the largest city in the county had twenty-five thousand people. Two centuries earlier, Russian fur traders charted the bay. I had read their translated travel journals while writing about local history. They named the bay *Zaleev Inditzov*, the Bay of Indians.

My father told me about the years he lived in Kodiak, Alaska, and fished the Bering Sea in open sailboats, traversing the Aleutians and seeing many of the historic landmarks of old Russian America. He'd also sailed into Vladivostok once in the winter in the 1930s aboard an American merchant marine ship.

What began as a simple curiosity about a few Russian fur-trader diaries and my father's stories turned into a full-blown obsession. A stack of books ranging from Tsarist wars to Soviet science fiction, Tolstoy to Yevtushenko, and two years of Russian language study culminated in a trip to the USSR.

I'd traveled extensively in North America over the previous ten years, visiting more than forty states, hitchhiking coast to coast three times, driving my truck to the Mexico-Guatemala border and back, motorcycling the five thousand—mile Trans-Canada Highway, traveling the Caribbean, but I'd never been to the other side of the world.

I thought it would be a shock to just fly from the redwoods to Red Square. Instead, I wanted to slowly immerse myself into this journey, approach the Soviet Union by ship from the east and ride the Trans-Siberian Express across the continent. I'd read several books about that legendary train ride. I planned to stop at Siberian towns and cities, see Lake Baikal, get a sense of the vastness that Siberia and Russia represented by riding the rails from Nakhodka to Moscow, and then continue south, into Ukraine.

That last afternoon at sea, I watched the approaching dark coastline of the Soviet Far East slowly materialize into rocky bluffs, capes, and hills of green grass. An ivory-colored lighthouse appeared near the entrance to Nakhodka Harbor as a rose glow reflected in the clouds toward the end of the day.

Two sailors stood near the anchor winch. Their Russian conversation faded in and out beneath the deep rumble of ship's engines, and the sound of the bow wash as the *Khabarovsk* broke through the waves.

I wondered how Soviets would react to an American traveling alone, since nearly all foreigners visited the USSR in groups or with guides. My entire trip had been arranged by a private travel agency in San Francisco that specialized in setting up solo itineraries for Soviet immigrants who wanted to return home to visit family and friends.

I was able to arrange two months of independent travel, including cities, small towns, camp areas, motels and hotels, a rental car, and second-class train tickets. There would be no official exhibits or official tours, just two months of self-discovered experiences across a vast foreign land. I wanted to drive on country roads, see the backstreets, meet strangers, and eat in public diners.

The Soviet Union defied comprehension. Spanning eleven time zones, its fifteen republics embodied more than one hundred languages and a variety of lifestyles based on European, Middle Eastern, Arctic, and Asiatic cultures. Traveling for two months in the USSR would not unravel any Soviet political mysteries. I would only touch a thread of a deeply layered and complex society.

But hidden away, there was another creative element that provoked my travel to the Soviet Union. I'd been playing music in Humboldt County for almost ten years in a local band, touring the Pacific Northwest club scene. I'd also seen Carl Sagan on a TV show talking about the possibility of the U.S. and USSR linking their space programs for a trip to Mars; instead of living in fear of mutual destruction, people would have a reason to imagine a shared mission together, a shared hope for the future, beyond the scope of everyday life.

I believed that music could do the same thing. I'd written a few songs—including one called "Journey to The Red Planet"—and translated them into Russian. I hoped to meet musicians to play with. I had those songs in my back pocket when I walked down the gangplank of the *Khabarovsk* that day in Nakhodka.

I was riding the crest of a twenty-five-year wave of fear and fantasy. All the dreams and nightmares I'd had about the USSR were behind me. By sunset, I would be aboard the Trans-Siberian Express.

It's Warm in Siberia

I stood in line at a small food kiosk on a Siberian rail station platform, entranced by the sounds and smells of a rainy morning at Shimanovsk Station, near the Chinese-Soviet border. Across the rail yard, near a pile of concrete ties, a dozen workers stood around a bonfire. Some of the crew wore heavy, quilted jackets and their pants tucked into tall black leather boots.

Rain sprinkled lightly on my face and puddled on the concrete platform. The smell of hot steel brakes and rail-bed creosote mingled with drifting bonfire smoke and burning coal. It had never occurred to me to wonder how the air might smell in a Siberian rail town during a summer rainfall.

When I awoke that morning aboard the train, the landscape of Siberia looked familiar, like the inland mountains and valleys of the Pacific Northwest. The seven-foot-square, second-class cabin seemed stuffy. I looked at the other bunks, where an old man and the young Soviet soldier I'd talked to the night before were still asleep. I was in the USSR.

The kiosk line moved slowly. My mind raced as my turn came, trying to figure out what I wanted to buy and to remember the Russian word for it. I felt nervous speaking Russian in such hurried situations. Unfamiliar words and slang expressions would fly past my ears unrecognized. People would look a little dumbfounded at some of my Russian language expressions, then smile in amused appreciation for attempting their language. All my classroom confidence had vanished.

"*Pomidor, pomidor, pomidor,*" I said to myself, practicing the word for tomato. At the kiosk window, an old woman in a long, flowered dress moved quickly, taking orders, and lining up the items on the worn wooden counter. The man in front of me filled a netted bag with food.

Since leaving the eastern seaport of Nakhodka two days before, the Trans-Siberian Express had stopped at many towns along the tracks, sometimes for only five minutes. Passengers would disembark and hurriedly buy local food from vendors who lined the station platforms, then jump back aboard. I'd studied their patterns. Now I was out there trying to buy food like the locals. I glanced at the train to make sure it wasn't creeping out of the station. I didn't want to be left in Shimanovsk without a passport or luggage. My cabin was near the end of the train, a long way from the station kiosks.

The conductors stood waiting along the platform with their yellow signal flags in hand. They eyed their watches. The mechanics were out from under the train. I was about ready to run for my car.

"*Da, shto vwee xotitya?*" Yes, what do you want? The old woman waited patiently for my order. I was thinking chicken but said cookies by mistake. She went for the cookies.

"*Nyet, nyet,*" I corrected. "*Cureetsa!*" She pulled a whole bird out of a pile of boiled chickens, hoisting it by the leg. She didn't hesitate at my awkwardness.

"*Nyet, palovina!*" Half a chicken. She spun around and grabbed half a cold chicken, quickly wrapping it up in some heavy, green paper. Breakfast in Siberia.

"Give me some of the cookies, too, please."

She took another piece of paper and effortlessly rolled a cone the size of a small megaphone, filling it with a dozen star-shaped shortbreads.

"Four carrots, two tomatoes, one bread, that's all!" Her aged fingers slid the small black beads of an abacus up and down the wooden shafts. The beads and shafts were shiny and worn from countless tabulations.

"Three rubles and twenty kopecks." About four dollars. She was as quick as a cash register.

She slowed her pace and smiled. The dark wrinkles on her face spoke of many Siberian seasons. Her eyes were a striking Caribbean light green. I thanked her and gave her the money. She told me she'd grown the vegetables in her garden.

"*Shastleevway,*" she said, wishing me good fortune. Her eyes sent a shimmer of warmth through me. Then she turned and hurriedly took the next person's order.

With my hands full of food, I sprinted the length of Shimanovsk Station, reaching my car a minute before the yellow flags fell.

The Trans-Siberian Express moved swiftly through the Khilok River Valley. I leaned against an open window frame and peered out across fields of wheat and grass to distant mountains. Rounded haystacks resembling huts dotted the Asian countryside. The white linen window curtains whipped near my face.

I turned to find my cabinmate, Pavel, behind me. We'd been sitting knee-to-knee for the last couple of days, armed with pens, paper, and a dictionary, trying to tell our life stories.

Pavel, in his late twenties, had brush-cut blond hair combed straight back, and glacial blue eyes that never seemed to blink. He didn't speak English.

"*Eta ochen kraseevwee, da?*" It's very beautiful, yes?

"Yes, I really like the countryside."

Our second-class compartment consisted of four bunks, two overhead and two below. A small table was positioned below a large window between the lower bunks that Pavel and I occupied. First-class compartments were the same size, but with just two lower bunks. I chose second class, thinking I'd meet more people that way, and I wasn't wrong. But I had deliberately avoided the Soviet Railway's more spartan third-class accommodations—six bunks, wide open, no window, no door.

I couldn't see enough of Siberia. I'd been staying awake into the early morn-

ing hours, just for a glimpse of an illuminated window or the station lamps that created shadows of travelers milling about rail station platforms. Rail bridges and tunnels sparkled like cities in the darkness, surrounded by flood lights, fences, towers, and armed guards. The Mongolian border was just a hundred and fifty miles to the south.

"*Posmotri!*" Look! Pavel pointed to an older man walking along a dirt path near a small creek, carrying a fishing pole in one hand and a string of fish in the other. He wore an old suit, rubber boots, a shirt buttoned to the neck, and a small woven cap. His eyes were fixed straight ahead as if he didn't notice the train hurtling across the Siberian countryside.

"That man knows a good life," Pavel yelled, his hair whipping in the wind. I started to say something just as an eastbound passenger train exploded past the open window, only six feet away. Instantly, the panorama turned into an avalanche of steel. We stepped back from the blast of hot air and exploding noise.

"*Eta gromki!*" That's loud, he yelled. The train disappeared abruptly. Pavel and I moved back to the open window and felt the rush of summer air against our faces.

We stood at the window for nearly an hour. Every ten or fifteen minutes a freight or passenger train blew by on the busy rail line. Pavel periodically disappeared to have a cigarette in the car's designated smoking vestibule, where the cars coupled.

After years of Red Army paranoia, it seemed ironic that the first Russian I met was a soldier, an officer. Pavel had boarded the train two nights before, on his way home to Moscow after serving two years on the Chinese border. We didn't talk much that first morning, although I'd given him some carrots and bread to have with morning tea. His soft-spoken, unassuming manner made me comfortable. By the second day, we were talking for hours at a time. After struggling through a conversation, we'd sit back exhausted and look out the window, or read.

"I'll buy dinner tonight," Pavel insisted, waving his hand to dismiss any protest. We left for the dining car. Twenty-four rail car doors separated our cabin from the train's restaurant car. The cars lurched and rolled, forcing us to grab handholds as our feet tried to compensate for the motion.

I was sure I'd get something to eat with Pavel. The last few times I had ventured to the dining car by myself, I found the door locked and my watch ticking in the wrong time zone. I'd shake the door, and the waiter would hold his wristwatch up to the window and point at the dial, shaking his head no.

The Trans-Siberian Express existed in its own tunnel of time, set to Moscow clocks. The train would roll into a town where the station clocks would show it was six o'clock in the morning, while train clocks pointed to midnight. Sometimes even the date confused me. At one end of the USSR, children were going to bed, and eleven time zones eastward, workers were pausing for a midday tea break the next morning. I'd given up trying to figure out when the dining car would be open.

The first couple of nights on the train, I'd survived with the help of a short, rotund Russian woman who walked the corridors, calling out, "*Koosheet! Koosheet! Xotitye koosheet?*" To eat! To eat! Do you want to eat? She carried a wire basket stacked with metal dishes of warm meat, potatoes, gravy, and brown bread. It cost fifty kopecks a plate, about seventy-five cents.

The dining car hummed with Russian conversation, kitchen noise, and Soviet radio playing an occasional, classic Russian romance melody floating melancholically through the car. A waiter with a small moustache and greasy hair seated Pavel and me at the last empty table. I studied the Cyrillic descriptions on the four-page menu for a few minutes while he and Pavel spoke.

"I'll have fish," I pointed to the word *reeba* on the second page.

"*Reeba nyet*," the waiter replied. No fish.

Pavel leaned across the table and placed his hand over the menu. "He says there is only one dinner."

That was simple. The menu was only a formality. Several minutes later, the waiter returned with a pitcher of ice water, cucumber and tomato salads, brown bread, and plates full of meat and potatoes out of a stew pot. I was reminded of the dinners my grandmother used to serve on her farm in the Sacramento Valley. Only the banging screen door and the scent of corn silage and alfalfa were missing.

"Nraveetsa?" Pavel wondered if I liked the dinner. "When you come to Moscow, I would like to take you out to one of my favorite restaurants."

As we ate, the dining car sliced through a sea of green grass that spread into the valley. I was surprised by the abundance of agriculture in Siberia. Every day, farms appeared. In many areas, men and women cut the tall grasses by hand, swinging long scythes in steady, rhythmic, ponderous motions.

Earlier in the day, Pavel had attempted to describe the Soviet agricultural system to me. His appreciation for rural life reminded me of an old saying I'd heard: "Scratch a Russian, find a farmer."

With a ballpoint pen, he sketched two big boxes that he labeled *sovxoz* and *kolxoz*, two different kinds of government farms. He drew dozens of tiny stick farmers standing alongside tiny bushels of wheat with many arrows pointing toward the government box. But there also seemed to be a lot of stick farmers with ruble signs in their back yards, earned from small, private gardens.

I sketched Pavel an oversimplified view of our farm system. Independent, small stick farmers sent produce to the public market. Off to the side, a large banking box took a lot of the stick farmers' profit and sometimes the farm. The government box gave big farms extra money so they wouldn't grow anything. Pavel shook his head without understanding. I told him most Americans didn't understand it, either.

Near the end of our meal, we were joined by two foreign travelers we'd met. A Japanese mountaineer, on his way to see the Pamir Mountains, with peaks exceeding twenty-thousand feet, in Soviet Central Asia, and a young Austrian on his way home after traveling across the United States.

The four of us spoke awkwardly, translating from English to German to Russian and back again so everybody could understand. The Austrian's English amused me, especially when he talked about the bears in Yellowstone Park.

"Yahs, vee ver in dee park, and dee ranger said to look out fer dee beers. Dot deez beers vill come to us vit der noses to bite down. So vee ver much concerned to avoid dee beers."

He kept cocking one eye at my laughter. Pavel gave the German version of the "beer" story a serious listen. He spoke German as a second language.

"*Poyekhali.*" Let's go. The waiter had cleared the table and brought change for a ten-ruble bill. The dining car was closed. After our dinner, Pavel and I sat on our bunks, enjoying the last of the light. On a dirt road alongside the train, a barefoot youngster pedaled an oversized bicycle near a cluster of village homes. Huge piles of firewood rivaled the size of some of the houses. Outside, the temperature was warm, but the massive wood piles foreshadowed a long winter.

The car steward knocked, asking if we wanted tea.

"*Dobray vyecher. Chaigh xotitye?*"

We both nodded. He used his hip to slide the door open, carrying tall glasses of hot black tea in ornate silver-handled glass holders. The steward, a pleasant man in his fifties, always wanted to know if everything was going all right for me.

"Tomorrow morning, at five o'clock, you get off the train at Irkutsk, right?" Pavel asked.

"*Da, pyat chasov,*" I confirmed.

I didn't look forward to getting off the train. I was just getting used to my surroundings, and I had attached myself to Pavel. He was the first Russian I'd come to know, and we had good rapport.

Since first seeing the Soviet coast emerging from the mists, when I was still aboard the *Khabarovsk*, I had felt as if I were being swallowed by something enormous. After four days and nights aboard the train, crossing a continent peppered by wooden villages with names like Chichatka and Amazar, we were still thousands of miles east of Moscow. By comparison, it would take Amtrak just three days to go coast to coast across America. I was a tiny speck in the middle of Siberia. But Pavel lived here. He knew the way out.

"I'd prefer to go on the train with you all the way to Moscow."

"That would be interesting," Pavel mused, "then I could show you the Union.

I would like that." Pavel referred to "the Union" in the same manner Americans used "the States."

Late in the evening, long after the city lights of Ulan-Ude had faded behind the train, Pavel reached into his leather briefcase and pulled out a bottle of Russian vodka. He set the bottle on the table along with a small loaf of brown bread. The red, white, and blue *Russkaya* label looked inviting.

"I bought this to celebrate coming home," he said. "It's been two years. And this time here with you is very good." He poured the vodka into our empty tea glasses after rinsing them out at the fountain in the corridor.

"*Nawsh druzhba!*" To our friendship.

"*Cherez fsyo vremya!*" For all time, I added.

I followed Pavel's lead, drinking the vodka in one motion, then eating a piece of brown bread. The rhythmic movements and deliberate eye contact with each toast made drinking more like a ritual than a casual cocktail. We sat back in our bunks and grinned at each other.

I tried to picture Pavel in his Soviet Army officer's uniform, since he wore civilian clothes on the train. I thought of my cousins in their military uniforms and told Pavel how strange it was to be sitting with a Soviet soldier after a lifetime of believing they were the enemy.

"*Ya znaiyou eta choostva.*" He echoed that feeling. I was the first American he'd ever met.

"Do you think our countries will have a war someday?" I asked.

Pavel stared at me without blinking.

"No. I don't think there will be a war. It can't happen." He cupped his hands together, flexing both arms in an arm-wrestling pantomime. "Our countries are like two strong men wondering who is strongest."

Pavel smiled, and after pouring another round, he sat up to the laminate table and sketched an angry Russian Cossack with big teeth, glaring eyes, and a star on his fur cap. He grinned while drawing the character, then held it up for me to inspect.

"Perhaps this is what Americans think Russians look like?" He sketched a second figure. A villainous Uncle Sam in a top hat of stars and stripes.

"And this is what Americans look like, yes?"

We both laughed.

I soon discovered that once a bottle of vodka was opened in Russia, it was all or nothing. Each time our glasses were emptied after a toast, Pavel refilled them. The first two were easy. But as we got toward the bottom of the bottle, I was starting to see stars. My head was swimming as the train roared through the night landscape.

Long after midnight, I remember Pavel painstakingly removing the vodka label from the empty bottle. Then he opened the window, letting in a blast of cold night air, and threw the bottle out somewhere between Selenginsk and Babushkin. He reached over and clasped my hand. We held on for a few seconds, looking at each other. There was nowhere else in the world I wanted to be at that moment. As the lights and roar of another train flashed by, Pavel inscribed a personal wish to me on the back of the red, white, and blue label, between the brown glue stripes.

> Zhon!
> I would very much like that we reminisce and travel across Russia and the Soviet Union. You have a long time to be here. I hope this isn't your last visit.
>
> Pavel

Five o'clock in the morning came quickly. The steward pried me from my bunk and carried my bags off the train in the darkness. I could tell he felt bad about having to dump me at the station in such a rush. I could barely stand up, and I had a headache. But he had to get me off the train. Pavel sat up and shook my hand one last time, chuckling at my disorientation. I hadn't slept very well. All night long, Siberian rail joints had clattered beneath my pillow like empty vodka bottles. Now I stood all alone in the dawn hour as the Trans-Siberian Express rolled out of Irkutsk Station toward the west.

"*Chaigh ili kofyay?*" Tea or coffee, asked the Irkutsk waitress. I stared down at an egg that was propped up and moving slightly on my plate.

"*Chaigh.*" I ordered the black tea. I drank half a dozen cups and ate some brown bread. I couldn't face the egg. I left it sitting on its porcelain stand, unshelled. My hangover needed to go for a walk.

I wandered into downtown Irkutsk and found an open-air *reenoak*, a farmer's market. Several hundred shoppers browsed the fresh produce, buying everything from beans and watermelons to meat pies and flowers. By now the summer heat was at full blast. My clothes stuck to me in the heat and humidity. Siberia felt like Florida. Maybe it was a combination of direct sun and nausea, but I felt panicky and disoriented. All I could hear was shoe leather scuffing on concrete. No boom boxes, no shouts, no traffic, nothing, just loud shuffling feet. I was used to noisy, American crowds.

I bought two apples from a farmer and retreated to a residential area of nineteenth-century housing flats. Their carved and oiled wood exteriors gave the neighborhood a frontier elegance. The street was lined with large shade trees.

A little boy with a butch haircut, glasses, and a striped T-shirt, pushed a toy Soviet tank through a mud puddle while making motor sounds with his lips. Around another corner, a construction worker blasted away at the street with an air hammer that sounded like it was inside my head. I found a quiet city park.

The small sign looked insignificant fastened on the side of the old two-story building, facing down a narrow concrete walkway. *Stolovaya*, a cafeteria for the people. A dozen wooden steps led up to a plain entrance that looked more like a fire exit. I watched a few people come and go before venturing in.

The door slammed behind me. A twenty-five-foot-high faded yellow ceiling echoed the sharp clatter of dishes. The pungent smell of fried and boiled food permeated the dimly lit room. I waited in line behind a dozen people, copying the man in front of me when he reached for a tray.

A log home in downtown Irkutsk

My outstretched plate met with a violent splat. Fish, I thought. I didn't want to ask.

Behind the counter, an agitated, large, redhaired woman in a tall white chef's hat, looking like a logging camp cook, moved with ferocity, shaking her serving spoon, shouting orders in Russian to the kitchen help, slamming big kettles into place, and just daring someone to complain. I quickly gathered up some buckwheat and a bowl of borscht. With brown bread, tea, and a cheese crepe, lunch totaled seventy kopecks, about a dollar.

I found an unoccupied table and spread out my dishes. A small squadron of flies showed up, but they sat politely off to the side of the plate and waited.

An anxious man in work clothes sat down across from me. After a few minutes, I initiated a conversation. The text-book phrase spilled from my lips as awkwardly as if I'd knocked over a glass of water on the table. "Hello there, by what profession are you occupied?" The man looked up surprised.

"*Rabotayou na mabyelnoi fabrika.*" He worked in a furniture factory. "You are a foreigner. Where do you come from?"

"California. I'm a tourist." I was glad I knew the word for furniture.

"California? You are a tourist? And you eat here?" He made a sweep of the room with his bread hand.

"Right. I want to meet people. This is more interesting than the hotel."

The man grinned.

"*Kak vas zavoot?*" I asked him his name, another well-rehearsed line.

"My name's Mosha."

He was on his lunch hour from a small factory. Most of the forty or so people surrounding us were workers, except for a colorfully dressed Romani woman wearing an abundance of silver jewelry. She sat in the corner talking to herself and taking occasional swipes at the air.

"What do you think of the Soviet Union?" Mosha asked.

That was a tough question since I'd been there less than a week. I told him that three-penny streetcar rides and hospitals without cash registers seemed impressive but that I didn't really know much. Mosha seemed satisfied with my answer. I told him I was having a good time, despite a hangover.

He quizzed me on the cost of cars, bread, and apartments in the States, and weighed my replies against twenty-kopeck Russian loaves and twelve-rubles-a-month apartments. Mosha decided that he was better off living in the USSR. He bid me good day with a handshake and returned to work. I think he left still puzzled why I was there.

The lunch was good, except for the fish. I was having a problem with the fish. Maybe it was a bad day to force down a strong, slimy substance. On the second bite, my lunch almost returned to the tray. I covered the fish with my napkin and slipped out the door.

I walked all day in ninety-degree heat until my mouth felt like cotton and my feet ached. All I wanted was something cold. Behind some plate glass windows, I noticed two rows of long, open freezers in a store. I walked inside. Small, colorful packages filled the freezers, and the Russian word for ice cream, *morozhenoye*, was written on each wrapper.

Russian ice cream was famous. I'd read somewhere that in Moscow alone people ate 170 tons of ice cream a day, even in the winter.

I wondered if they would be ice cream sandwiches with chocolate cookie backings? Vanilla? Maybe the green packages were mint? I didn't care what flavor it was, as long as it was cold. I picked one and held a handful of kopecks out to the cashier. She took fifteen kopecks from my change.

I found a riverside bench and peeled open my first Russian ice cream bar. It had a strange coarse texture. I eyed the orange brick of ice cream thinking citrus, then took a large bite.

Fish! Salted fish!

I gagged and spit it out on the sidewalk, then ran for a nearby drinking fountain to rinse the hake sherbet, or whatever it was, out of my mouth. The aftertaste was horrible.

Morozhenoye must mean more than one thing. Or the Russians had one flavor that Baskin-Robbins didn't. A closer review of the orange wrapper revealed illustrations of little fish jumping around the word *moriye*, meaning the sea. It turned out to be frozen fish paste for cooking.

I walked back over to the park bench and found a dog licking the mess off the sidewalk. Most dogs would have rolled in something that repulsive. I still had the orange wrapper and its contents in my hand.

"*Itee sudah sabachka.*" Here, little dog.

The scrubby wire-haired mutt finished off the fish paste.

Two days later, I ventured by hydrofoil ferry down the Angara River from Irkutsk to Lake Baikal.

It was a Soviet national holiday, and the public pier had been jammed with people that morning. I'd stood in line for more than two hours to buy my ticket, having chosen to take the public ferry instead of a tourist boat. From my place in line, I had seen the tourist boat arrive, load its passengers, and depart in an orderly fashion without delay—no lines, no wait, and no Soviet passengers.

It was a different story when the public ferry arrived, and the Soviet passengers, who had been calmly waiting to board, began pushing and shoving as they rushed for the gangplank. I was swept aboard in a mob of passengers on holiday, many sporting colorful short-sleeved shirts, sandals, and dark glasses and carrying cameras.

The ferry, known as a Racketa, produced an enormous roar from its twin diesel engines, which generated a thousand horsepower, lifting it out of the water on hydrofoils and speeding at forty knots down the river. Its profile was futuristic Like an aviator, the captain sat in a glassed-in cockpit perched on top of the fuselage. Sweeping curved-glass windows wrapped around the forward passenger area like a solarium, and each side of the ninety-foot craft was lined with oversized, airplane-styled windows. Fins and airfoils protruded from the hull in various places. The vessel appeared half ship and half aircraft as it rose on its foils and roared down the Angara. My ears were ringing as I stood at the open stern and watched rooster tails rise from the water. It was a fast trip to the shore of Baikal.

Once departing the ferry at the village of Listvyanka, I wandered along the shore and found a big rock to sit on and enjoy the calm of a summer day beside the deepest lake in the world. The ringing in my ears subsided.

Then a splash caught my attention.

Beneath the frigid waters of Lake Baikal, I saw the milky white form of a swimmer. He burst to the surface with a scream, thrashing madly to keep his muscles and joints from seizing in the cold of one of the world's chilliest lakes. He swam farther out into the lake, then paused to tread water and look back at the beach. He noticed me sitting on the rocky outcropping and yelled in Russian, "Come swimming! For your health!"

I just waved to him and shrugged my shoulders. He dove under water again. A faint haze hung in the air, distorting the pine forested mountains on the far shore. Lake Baikal was far from the encapsulated tension of tiny train compartments and crowded city streets. I enjoyed the quiet.

"*Zdarovaya! Zdarovaya!*" The swimmer was persistent. "*Xaroshaya voda!*" He was still yelling about health and good water.

I waved at him a second time and shouted a polite refusal. Two women walked nearby, and I felt self-conscious yelling at the lake in Russian. The swimmer headed for shore.

I knew the cold water would have felt invigorating. It was a lousy day to be wearing thick black corduroy pants. I wished I'd brought shorts and a towel. Baikal was one of the great natural wonders of the USSR, similar in national stature to the U.S. Grand Canyon. It is the deepest and largest freshwater lake in the world, holding more water than all the Great Lakes combined.

"Come here! Come here!" The swimmer was vigorously drying off, shouting and motioning for me to join him. His persistence made me wary, but I climbed off the rock and walked down the beach to see what he wanted.

"You are a foreigner? Yes?" He eagerly thrust out his cold hand to mine.

He talked so rapidly that my Russian was rendered useless. I guessed that he was about thirty-five. He was short, almost elfin, with twinkling dark eyes and large ears. He tried to describe with gestures what I might miss from his rapid speech. My apprehension suddenly disappeared. I liked this man. I told him where I was from.

"*Amerikanetz!*" he exclaimed, pumping my arm enthusiastically. "Good to meet you. Very good." He continued his friendly blitz of words. At best, I was on the outer edge of deciphering his speech, but I nodded eagerly, laughed, and pretended I understood everything.

"Where is your group?" he asked. "What, no group? You're alone? Very good! Very good! An American traveler alone in Russia! At Lake Baikal! And you speak Russian." His excitement grew. Then a serious expression froze his face, and he reached for my elbow. "You are the first American I have met. But do not be afraid. I am not a communist!"

I burst out laughing. He paused with an inquisitive look, then shook my hand for the third time, and introduced himself as Anatoly. I asked him to speak more slowly. He tried, but his runaway energy was just redirected into gestures as he simultaneously buttoned his shirt, put on his shoes, and carried on two conversations, one describing the natural wonders of Lake Baikal and the other about a school he attended in Irkutsk.

Anatoly stopped his monologue abruptly, pointed to the hills, and said, "Come to my house. Please, be my guest."

When I said yes, his chatter reached a new level of excitement. A moment of doubt surfaced, and I wondered if Anatoly was a lunatic. But as we walked together, I remained comfortable with him. He managed to speak more slowly and simply, although the urgency remained.

We walked through the village of Listvyanka, following a rutted dirt road into the hills far above the lake. The steep, green landscape reminded me of the inland hills of Northern California. Roughly fenced yards and little wooden homes along the dirt road could easily be the wooded neighborhoods of rural Humboldt or Mendocino county.

About two hundred feet ahead of us, an older woman in a yellow and black polka-dot print dress stood in front of the gate to a small house. She waved and quickly disappeared behind a high wooden fence.

"That's my mother," Anatoly said, as we neared the blue and white house.

Before following him through the gate, I stopped and looked back down the little valley to the peaked roofs of Listvyanka and beyond to Lake Baikal. The breeze rustled trees and hillside grasses, and a large shrub hung over the fence, spilling brilliant pink blossoms.

I walked along a path of boards and ducked my head to enter a lopsided pantry. The floor was tilted, the ceiling slanted, and trapezoidal window frames appeared to float lazily in the walls, like a Salvador Dali creation. I doubted that a plumb bob or level had been consulted in the construction of this room.

The aroma of fresh bread and the mustiness of old furniture greeted me. I noticed that the rest of the house followed more conventional parallel and perpendicular lines. Anatoly's mother stood with her back to us at the woodburning cook stove as she prepared a hot lunch. She turned for a moment to greet me with a warm smile and hello before resuming her work. She was slicing hot bread.

On the outskirts of Lystvanka at Lake Baikal

An older man had been relaxing at the kitchen table with a cigarette in hand, staring out a paned window into the vegetable and flower garden. He appeared to be in his mid-seventies. His strong face was scored by long, deep lines. Anatoly introduced me to his father. He stood up, shook my hand, and offered me a chair at the table next to him. His name was Anton.

I set my shoulder bag on the cracked linoleum floor. Anatoly bustled around, hanging up our coats, clearing off the table, and telling his parents how we'd met. During this brief account, Anton listened and nodded from behind his cigarette.

Anatoly's mother, Galina, walked between the stove and the table, delivering plates and bowls filled with food, and making sure that I was comfortable. In a matter of minutes, the table was covered with an enormous dinner.

Anton lifted the lid from a large yellow bowl and slowly enunciated the word for its contents. "*Pir-osh-ki.*" He accented each syllable. "Very good to eat."

"I know about *piroshki*," I replied. "What kind are they?"

Anton grinned and looked at Galina and Anatoly. "This American knows about Russian food," he mused. "Yes?" He turned back to me. "Mushroom and cabbage. Do you know these other things?" He motioned to the various dishes covering the table.

My Russian language ability was limited, but food was a topic I knew. With a small ray of confidence, I scanned the table. The homemade bread was still warm and closest to me. I pointed to it: "*kleb*." A plate of garden tomatoes and cucumbers: "*pomidori e ogurtzi*." A bowl of sour cream: "*smyetana*." The cabbage soup: "*shchi*." The cheese: "*sear*." Butter: "*maslo*." I came to the last plate, fish: "*reeba*." I had passed the test. Anatoly slapped my shoulder. Galina's round face broke into a smile. She insisted that we eat right away before the dinner got cold, but Anton interrupted her.

Anton in his garden

"Wait. You are the first American to come to our house. You speak to us in Russian, you know of our food, and today is a holiday. First, a drink."

Anton snapped his index finger to his throat, a Russian gesture that indicates the intent to share a drink. He rustled around in a cupboard behind his chair and came up with a bottle of dry red wine from the Georgian Republic. Anatoly filled three water glasses. Galina didn't drink.

Anton picked up his glass. With a resolute voice he toasted to health, "Na zdarovaya!" Anatoly and I, holding our glasses up, repeated the phrase. I put the glass to my nose, swirled the wine to release its bouquet, and washed a small sip over my tongue. I became aware that Anatoly and his father were both watching me anxiously. Their empty glasses were already on the table. This was not the California wine country, it was Siberia. I gulped down the Georgian red, then set the glass on the table with theirs. They looked relieved.

When we started lunch, Galina hovered over my plate like a hen, prodding me to try more *piroshki*, more fish, more soup. Another cup of tea?

When I thought I could eat no more, she brought in three large bowls with different wild berries in each, a plate of cookies, and another pot of black tea. Anton picked up a cookie and dipped it in his tea.

"Many days I see foreigners at the lake," he said. "They walk in their groups and talk their own languages. Mostly Europeans and Japanese, a few Americans. But you are the first foreigner to come to my house."

Across the table from where I sat, the multi-paned window looked out onto a flower garden abundant with pink cosmos and colorful sweet peas. The entire garden was in bloom. As I ate blackberries and sour cream, I thought about the tourists I had seen that morning who had purchased the expensive tickets to avoid all the people. What were they doing now? What would be their impressions of Lake Baikal? "... Lake Baikal contains twenty percent of the world's fresh water supply ... is over five thousand feet deep and 350 miles long..." I quickly returned to the sunlit kitchen.

I noticed an old black and white photograph on the wall behind Anatoly. The framed image was of Soviet soldiers with Stalin standing in their midst.

"You are looking at this photograph? That's my father." He stood up and pressed his finger to the glass showing me a young officer with a straight back and a smooth, determined face. I glanced over at Anton, who appeared not to be listening. The garden view held his interest. His mind was elsewhere.

Anatoly continued, "I told you that I am not a communist, but my father is a communist. He was in the army when he was younger. World War II was a very hard time in Russia." Anatoly emphasized these last words. Anton's survival of four years of war on the Russian-German front as a field officer had probably put many of those deep lines in his face. I looked back to him. He sat motionless, a slow, tumbling cloud of smoke rising from his cigarette. Images of horror crept up in my mind—the Siege of Leningrad, hundreds of thousands of people starving to death, the Defense of Stalingrad, more than a million lives lost in bitter street fighting during the winter. Those realities seemed a long way from the warm, quiet Siberian cottage.

I wanted to say something meaningful to Anton but managed only a mundane question about how he liked Lake Baikal. He was silent for a moment, then replied that he enjoyed resting and being near the lake. "Here, at Lake Baikal, it is very quiet."

After we finished the tea and berries, Anatoly invited me to see the rest of the small house. A pantry, the large open-rafter kitchen and sitting area, and a sardine-can living room with a seven-foot ceiling. Anatoly led the way up a back staircase to the second-story bedroom.

On the stairs, I glanced at my watch and realized that the last ferry to Irkutsk was about to leave. Time had been a remote concern, but now a minor panic. Baikal Pier was three miles away. "Anatoly," I said pointing to my watch, "the last boat is in twenty minutes." Anatoly didn't flinch. He sat down on one of the three beds in the room. "No need to worry," he reassured me. "No problem. I must go to Irkutsk tonight, too. I have a bus ticket, and I will take you on the bus with me." The bus wouldn't leave for another two hours. My panic retreated.

In one corner of the bedroom, I spotted a wooden balalaika leaning against a wall. I asked Anatoly if I could play it. "You play the balalaika?" I told him no, but that I played a guitar.

My fingers strummed the oddly tuned, three-gut-stringed, triangular instrument. The music from the film *Doctor Zhivago* came to my mind. I plunked out a melody on the high string and found a simple pattern that kept the other two strings harmonious. My technique made the instrument sound more like a banjo.

"Come! I want you to play for my mother." Anatoly led me downstairs, through the lopsided pantry and into the fenced-in garden. Galina was sitting over a huge tub of freshly gathered mushrooms, cleaning and preparing them to preserve for the winter.

"Mother, listen! He plays the balalaika!" He found a seat for me on the porch, then proudly stepped back as if unveiling a new discovery.

Galina dropped her arms to her apron and squinted to see me in the sunlight. "You play the instrument?" she asked. I explained that I didn't, but that I played other stringed instruments. "Please play." The tone of her voice encouraged me.

I plunked away for several minutes, producing an American folk melody. Galina and Anatoly listened, applauding when I was done. They were being very polite. Anatoly said that his mother played the balalaika.

Galina playing her balaika in Lystvanka

"Then you must play for me." I handed the old wooden instrument over to her. She wiped her hands dry on her apron before taking it. Galina held the balalaika like a dear friend, adjusted the tuning pegs, and strummed a traditional

Russian song that brought the instrument's authentic sound to life. She began playing slowly, then increased the tempo with Slavic vigor until her right hand was a blur of sixteenth notes. The melody was a blending of folk simplicity with a hint of oriental mystery.

As I sat and listened to Galina play the balalaika, I felt I was touching the heart of Russia.

It was then that I began to understand a Russian word I had learned that is not easily translated into English and is difficult for a foreign mind to fathom. It describes the Russians' deep-rooted affinity for the land on which they have lived for more than a millennium. The word is *Rodina*—the motherland.

With a grin of satisfaction, Galina struck a resounding chord that finished her song and looked at me.

"Galina," I said, "Where did you learn to play music? You play so well."

She gently set the balalaika down in the grass, leaning its fretted neck against the house. "When I was six years old, I was given a balalaika." She reached into the tub of water and took out a large orange mushroom. "I learned to play by ear and from friends."

"That's how I learned," I replied. "No school, only in life."

She laughed, nodding at my remark. "That's very good to learn. Music and life."

Anatoly appeared with two large glasses of *kvas*, a Russian drink made from whole wheat bread fermented in water. When he told me it was *kvas*, my stomach took a turn. Two days before, I had stopped on an Irkutsk street corner after noticing several people with their noses to the sky, drinking an amber liquid that looked like beer. The vendor dipped a tall mug into a hundred-gallon *kvas* tank on wheels, and I drank it down. The first gulp was shocking. Nothing in America resembles *kvas*. Its taste lingers between sour apple juice and stale sourdough. I vowed it would never pass my lips again.

I thanked Anatoly for the tall glass of *kvas* and looked down at the small particles of soggy brown bread floating in murky water. He lifted his glass. "To health!" I wasn't so sure.

"To friendship!" I replied, drinking it down.

It was delicious. I told him it was much better than the street vendor's. He wrinkled his face at the notion of a vendor's *kvas* and pointed to his mother confidently. "She makes the best *kvas*." Anton came out of the house to join us in the garden.

Anatoly took the empty glasses back in and quickly returned with his small bag of books and clothes. He pointed to my watch and said that we should start walking for Listvyanka to meet the bus.

Galina set her mushrooms aside and handed Anatoly a large cloth bag filled with dozens of *piroshkis*, fresh cucumbers and tomatoes, cookies, and a container of berries. She kissed him on the cheek. Anton stood up, gripped my hand and wished me good fortune on my travels in the Soviet Union. He sat down again near a bush of sweet peas and lit another cigarette.

I turned to Galina. She reached out both hands to me and held mine for a moment. She smiled and said, "Thank you for coming to our home. Goodbye."

"A big thanks to you," I said, "To life and music!"

"Yes. To life and music," she repeated happily.

Anatoly held the gate open for me, and the next moment we were walking side by side down the dirt road toward Lake Baikal. In a matter of hours we would be back in the city of Irkutsk. Along the road we met a stooped old man with a white beard who shuffled along muttering hellos to us. A few wispy clouds had gathered on the jagged mountainous horizon to the east, but the sky to the west remained clear as the sun began to drop behind the hills where Anatoly's house stood. We stopped for a few moments to feel the last rays of sunlight.

The whole problem started late one afternoon, shortly after a young woman flagged down the bus and stole the driver's attention. She didn't look like a rural Siberian, with her long, painted nails, elaborate make-up, and high heels. I could see no houses or cars where she stood, only the forest and river.

Once she boarded the crowded yellow bus, the driver revved the engine, and we were back on the road. The driver's steel-gray eyes darted back and forth between the highway and the young woman. He insisted that she sit in a strange little seat bolted down next to his. I kept watching his eyes reflected in the wide rearview mirror.

He seemed to be driving faster now. I would have felt better if he'd had both hands on the wheel, but he kept reaching under his seat into a rumpled paper bag and passing candies to the woman. He'd say something to her and laugh at his own remarks. She seemed indifferent to his overtures, although she accepted the candy. He didn't offer any to me or to the older woman next to me, who had a bucket of berries tucked between her rubber boots.

I was returning to Irkutsk after a late afternoon swim in Lake Baikal. Since meeting Anatoly two days before, I'd regretted not diving into the lake. I had returned to Baikal to swim in the freezing water. I'd plunged beneath the surface, defying the frigid waters, exhilarated by the cold, clear fresh water.

I had swum for half an hour in the legendary lake, its crystal-clear water revealing a rocky underwater spectrum of ancient times. At one point I dove about ten feet beneath the surface to touch the bottom near the shoreline and discovered a smooth, aged bone fragment and brought it back to the surface. A small treasure. I emerged chilled from the waters and sat on the rocks looking out across Baikal to the east. The view had been extraordinary, with the sun casting a golden reflection across the expansive waters, the eastern shore miles in the distance. I had been glad the rocks along the beach were heated by the sun.

Now, as the bus jostled along the highway, my fingers ran over the smooth, time-sculpted bone I'd found lying on the lake bottom. A remembrance that would travel with me throughout my journey.

About fifteen minutes down the road, the driver swerved the bus off the highway and onto a smaller road that cut through a forest. I was startled. I think everyone aboard the bus was surprised. The passengers had been pretty quiet, but as soon as the bus veered onto the other road, the buzz of conversation swelled. The driver kept stealing side glances at his pretty passenger.

This was supposed to be the same bus that Anatoly and I had caught. Now we were headed in the opposite direction. What if we were going where foreigners weren't supposed to be? I wanted to get off.

Another bus was pulled over by the side of the road. The driver flagged us down and wanted to know what we were doing in this area. Our driver yelled back, "Ladna, everything's okay, don't worry about it." He slammed his window shut, and we took off again. The forest opened to fields. A few scattered buildings appeared in the distance. We whizzed by a pristine, white bus stop shelter, where someone had used a wide paint brush to slop on the bold word, MONTANA, in English. Graffiti artists from Missoula or what? Maybe a San Francisco 49ers fan.

I thought about asking the woman sitting next to me where we were going, but she didn't look very talkative. She was a big woman who stared resolutely straight ahead, never glancing at me or smiling. Her scarf was knotted tightly under her chin, and she took up quite a bit of the seat. I was pressed against the side of the bus.

"Irkutsk!" The bus driver announced.

Irkutsk maybe. I didn't recognize any of the streets or buildings. It was an old, dilapidated section of town. Most of the passengers got off the bus and disappeared down the sidewalks. I remained on the bus, hoping to see something that I recognized. There seemed to be a lot of grumbling, as if people had ended up in the wrong location. The young woman got off the bus, too, but then she returned to her seat with a small travel bag. The driver seemed pleased. I began to suspect that he was taking her on personal errands.

My mistake was to stay on the bus, hoping to see a familiar landmark. But the only thing I recognized was the low, sprawling skyline of Irkutsk as it disappeared to the east.

Next stop, I decided. We'd been back on the road about twenty minutes. Irkutsk city center lay far behind us. So I waited. And waited. The bus didn't stop. We drove straight into the Siberian countryside. The bus roared along, gobbling up the white lines as the driver continued to entertain his pretty blonde passenger. A road sign indicated "Angarsk, 40 km." The next city. The sun was ready to set.

I stood up and yelled over to the driver, motioning to a bus stop in the distance.

"*Sledooyoushe ostanovka.*" Next stop.

He looked up at me, surprised and distracted. So did the young woman. I got the immediate feeling that a Russian would have said that differently. The driver's glances ricocheted between the turnout and me standing beside him. The bus slammed to a stop. I jumped out and landed in the middle of Kansas somewhere. Shades of Dorothy and the Tin Man.

A straight highway disappeared over low hills and farmlands. The bus turned into a tiny puff of smoke beneath a heavy orange sunset.

I briefly admired the colorful ceramic tile designs that decorated the ornate bus stop shelter, but I didn't feel very optimistic about being stuck twenty-five miles out of Irkutsk at nightfall, surrounded by aggressive mosquitoes. Across the road, I tried sticking my thumb out to hitchhike. A couple of cars went by, but I think I was observed as a curiosity.

After a while, two young men walked up from a distant farm. One man's face and hands were as dark as the earth. He wore shoes, but no socks, a small woven cap, and work trousers held up by a length of rope. He carried the four-foot blade of a hand crosscut saw, without the handles. They had used those saws in Humboldt County to cut timber in the 1800s. His friend was in blue jeans with a nylon windbreaker tied onto an orange backpack. I asked when the next bus came through, which prompted the usual question of where I was from.

"California," I replied.

The guy with the crosscut saw paused, adjusted his hat a little, and looked down at his feet. He glanced at his partner with a slight grin, as if to say, "This guy's putting us on."

"What are you doing out here?" he questioned. I was wondering the same thing.

"*Nepravelna avtobus.*" The wrong bus. Another car went by. I stuck out my thumb. Rejected again.

The young man wearing the blue jeans took off his backpack and laid it in the gravel. "*Shto eta takoy?*" He asked what I was doing with my thumb up in the air. He imitated my roadside gesture as he spoke.

"Hitchhiking," I answered.

"Heeetch-haeekeeng?" he mimicked with awkward curiosity. I told him that in the U.S., if you stuck out your thumb you might get a ride. I didn't tell him that you might also get a bottle thrown at you.

The fellow with the saw blade stepped toward me with his weathered thumb in the air. He made an erasing motion with his other hand to nullify the protruding thumb.

"Here, is this." His hand flattened into a plane, with fingers tight together. He raised it chest high, then pumped up and down with a robotic motion as if patting a very tall dog on the head.

"Ah, hitchhiking in Siberia." I imitated his pumping hand. He nodded, approving of my style. Another car sped by, unfazed by my Russian gesture. It didn't surprise me. All the cars zooming along were small Soviet compacts. Most had three or four people in them. I also realized that I didn't appear as a single rider, standing next to these two characters with a crosscut saw and a loaded backpack.

We stood around the better part of an hour, swatting mosquitoes, talking, and watching the western horizon for the next bus. Drivers began switching on their headlights. I was surprised by my immediate rapport with both young men and their quick response to accommodate my level of Russian language. They spoke in simple terms, laughing and using their fingers to illustrate descriptions in the dust and gravel at our feet. Now, I was happy the bus had taken a different route, despite the mosquitoes.

Another car whizzed by.

"Heeetch-haeeekeeng." The fellow with the backpack tried out the word again, laughing at its strange sound and wiggling his thumb around.

Roadside entertainment.

As the night sky darkened, I gave up the notion of hitchhiking and decided that I'd eventually get back to Irkutsk if I stuck close to these two. The fellow with the cap worked as a laborer in a big *kolxoz* farm a few kilometers down the dirt road. His friend was a university student on summer vacation visiting friends in different areas of the country via the rail system. They were headed into Irkutsk to a store that evening.

Our conversation leapfrogged into an exchange of economic facts and figures, over wages, rent, consumer items, and transportation. The student, who lived in the big Soviet oil city of Baku in the Azerbaijan Republic, asked me about the long lines of slow-moving, bumper-to-bumper commuter traffic in America that he'd seen on Soviet TV.

"This is true?" he asked, quite amazed.

"*Da.*" I told him that American news clips showed long lines of Soviet shoppers standing motionless, waiting to buy food and consumer items. Our rural Siberian bus stop summit meeting also unearthed the fact that for the same amount of money, a Soviet teenager could either buy one Levi's outfit or travel across the country by rail five or six times. On the other hand, an American could buy one train ticket across the U.S., or half a dozen pairs of Levi's. That explained why denim jeans fluttered like national flags from American clothes lines and ten million travelers rode the Soviet rail system every day.

"*Avtobus!*" We spotted the running lights of an approaching bus. I pulled a few kopecks out of my pocket for the fare, but the man with the sawblade and hemp rope belt insisted on buying the tickets. We sat in the rear of the crowded bus. The lights of Irkutsk soon appeared to the east, a jewel in the midst of Siberian darkness.

Irkutsk was a quiet city at night. Little traffic and few people. I strolled through one of the old residential areas, along Gorky Street, feeling the cracks of an uneven sidewalk beneath my feet. The air was warm and still. Large, deciduous trees veiled amber streetlamps, casting long shadows. Open alleyways smelled of cats.

The sound of electric music drifted in and out, faintly, in the distance, then disappeared. I thought the music was coming from a home stereo. I stopped to listen. Nothing. Several windows showed light. I walked again. The music arose once more, glancing off walls, sliding beneath still trees.

I turned down another street. Cymbals and drums sounded louder. The ghostlike music resumed and dissipated several more times. I walked along the north bank of the Angara River and looked out across the wide expanse of dark water.

An open-air pavilion built on a narrow finger of land sparkled with flood lights, while a crowd danced to a Russian rock band. A concrete footbridge led out to the small peninsula.

It took me a few minutes to figure out that the concert was free, after tentatively walking through the entrance with a ruble in hand, thinking that someone would stop me.

The music was good, but a loud crackle in the speakers made it sound like they were singing over crumpling tinfoil. About three hundred young people moved conservatively on the wooden dance floor, offering sparse applause between numbers.

The band played three more songs, then, in one wave, the entire crowd exited the pavilion. It must have been rehearsed. Three hundred people don't disappear in sixty seconds without a sound. A group of six remained on the dance floor in front of the band. They were joking around and seemed more extroverted than the stoic crowd. The band returned for a strange two-song encore to the nearly empty pavilion. None of this made any sense to me.

When the band started to break down their gear, I hopped up onto the side stage to talk with one of the guitar players. I asked him about *"popyular plastinkies."* Popular records. With a surprised look, he rattled off the names of what sounded like a dozen characters from a Tolstoy novel.

His attention was distracted by the equipment teardown and other musicians. I had trouble grasping what he said, but he kept talking. We did manage to communicate a few shared images. In California or Siberia, rock and roll was rock and roll, a guitar was a guitar, and Lennon had rocked the world.

The concert stragglers wandered over and clustered around until the guitarist excused himself to help the other musicians who worked under the lights putting gear away.

"Vwee Americanetz." It came more as a confirmation than a question. Half a dozen hands reached out to meet me. The group introduced themselves with a blur of names. They were all college students. A few of the guys had obviously been drinking.

I had planned to wait around and talk some more with the musicians, but the students insisted I join them. No refusals. One reached for my shoulder bag and slung it over his arm. A young woman took my right arm, and a fellow called Sergei gripped my left arm. Off we went, out of the pavilion into the night, a cluster of seven. They laughed and made loud proclamations between a barrage of questions directed my way. I was caught in a human riptide with no idea where we were headed.

"*Egraesh* guitar?" Do you play guitar, the young woman named Katya asked. She carried a cheap, flat-top guitar slung over her back like a rifle, held in place by a length of rope.

"*Da.*"

The whole group immediately stopped. The guitar was thrust into my hands, and the friends huddled in front of me, leaning on each other's shoulders, waiting expectantly. I sang "Dark Hollow," an old country tune. They loved it. They would have loved anything sung in English.

After the song, we moved on. No one would let me carry anything. They all bunched together as before, and we continued over the concrete footbridge toward downtown Irkutsk. I wasn't used to such close physical contact in a group of people. Even my long-time friends moved at elbow's distance, except for greetings. Here, I'd noticed young women strolling together holding hands. Mothers and daughters, too. At one chess match in the park, two men casually rested their arms on a friend's shoulder while watching the game. I liked the friendly intimacy.

A night policeman in a long gray coat walked his beat along the promenade.

"Shh, shh," Sergei hissed. Everyone hushed into giggles and suppressed snorts of laughter. One of the young men, Serioza, broke off from the group and stopped to talk with the policeman for a few minutes. Boris, a big husky guy, kept trying to get his drunken arm around me. Sergei and Katya reprimanded him.

Lacking Serioza, we turned up Karl Marx Street, walking as a great twelve-legged spider. I was curious where we were headed.

"*Ne deleko,*" Sergei said, not very far.

We caroused along dark cobbled alleys and up a side street to a small, dimly lit park sandwiched between several four- and five-story apartment buildings. Eleven o'clock at night in Siberia, and everyone wore short-sleeved shirts.

Serioza soon showed up with two more friends and another guitar. He continued quickly across the park and through the double doors of one of the apartment buildings. He returned with a bottle of vodka and two water glasses. Boris kept sidling up next to me, reaching out with his big friendly paws and slurred phrases.

Sergei's cheekbones were wide and prominent, hinting at Cossack ancestry. "*Zhon,*" he said urgently, his tone riddled with anxiety. "What do American people think about Soviet Union? About war?"

"American people don't want war."

"We don't want war, either."

"Only friendship," Serioza insisted.

Their urgency sent shivers across my shoulders. My neck felt hot. "Would America drop the bomb a third time?" Their question stopped me.

Our sudden lunge toward world concern sent us on a depressing tumble. Everyone felt nervous living in the crosshairs of electronic guidance systems. I'd had the same conversations with friends at home.

"Tell people in America we Soviet people want peace. Peace and friendship!" Katya's voice rang with emotion.

A chorus of agreement echoed her statement. Serioza opened the bottle of vodka and poured a four- or five-ounce shot in each, handing them to Sergei and me.

"*Mir.*" Peace. We raised our glasses. It was a long way to the bottom. I grimaced a little from the taste, remembering the last night on the train with Pavel. A shower of sparks danced in my head. Everyone toasted to peace. Everyone but Boris. I knew he wanted peace, too, but I could hear him vomiting in the bushes. A small swig of vodka remained. I was the honored guest.

Sergei handed me a guitar and picked up the other one. He sang a Rus-

ЧЕЛОВЕК
Искренне Ваш
ПРИШЛА И ГОВОРЮ
ВИНА
ЛЕЙТЕНАНТА
НЕКРАСОВА

sian ballad. A chorus of voices joined in on what must have been a traditional tune. I accompanied them with a running arpeggio of melody. They asked me to play a song.

I strummed a fast tempo ska beat from a song I'd written in Jamaica. Now in Siberia, the chameleon rhythm took on the guise of a Slavic backbeat. Everyone clapped hands. Sergei and the others phonetically imitated the chorus line with me. They didn't know what they were singing, but they hummed over the rhythm. "Every living day, we must find a way, to better this life we're livin' in."

Then I tried the Russian translation of a song I'd written, called "We All Want the Future." The group tried to sing along, but it was too awkward. People struggled with my choice of Russian words, which apparently didn't make sense. Soon the other guitar player stopped playing and just watched. I felt like I was singing gibberish.

We played songs until after midnight. The music had lifted our mood. Boris tried awkwardly to relate to me by periodically grabbing the guitar neck. Each time, Katya patiently led him away and talked with him. He'd nod agreeably then return. I noticed that few lights remained on in the surrounding apartments, but no one had thrown their shoe at us for playing music.

"*Zhon*," Sergei tapped his watch. "It's getting late. Katya and I will walk you to the hotel." They wanted to meet me the next night, but I had a train ticket for five o'clock in the morning at Irkutsk Station. After an enthusiastic round of handshakes, good lucks, and goodbyes from the rest of the group, we headed out of the park. Boris decided to accompany us.

The four of us locked arms and set off down deserted sidewalks. I thought the world was a fine place at that moment. The vodka had left me feeling warm and lightheaded.

We passed beneath the unbroken shadow of large trees. I wondered if the city had been built around the forest. When we reached the hotel, Katya and Sergei wished me a peaceful night. "*Spakoine noche!*" Boris mumbled something and shook my hand with what felt like a pair of vise grips. I started for the dark hotel.

I was about halfway across the parking lot when I heard footsteps running toward me. I turned and was blindsided by a flying tackle and drunken laughter. Boris had returned.

"Boris, *nyet*." I tried to wriggle free of his grip, but he'd gotten both arms around me in a wrist lock. I looked around, hoping that Katya or Sergei would come out of the shadows to save me, but they were nowhere in sight. Boris tightened his grip and dug in with his feet, the whole time laughing and repeating, "*Zhon*, let's go to my home. You will be my guest."

I tried to refuse, but my head spun from the vodka. Boris and I stumbled around out in the parking lot until my resistance disintegrated into laughter. We were a fine pair. I agreed to visit his home. Boris was ecstatic. It was about one o'clock in the morning. We headed off arm in arm.

Boris lived about ten blocks from the hotel. We turned off the main street down a dark, unpaved alley. Cats darted around in the shadows, ducking behind a row of trash cans. At the end of the alley, an enormous hardwood tree loomed over the back section of an old, two-story green house.

He fumbled with a key, opened the door, and ushered me into a small three-room flat, an addition onto the back of the big house. Boris told me his wife had gone to visit her mother for the week. He slid a chair over for me to sit on.

The apartment was untidy but not a disaster. An entrance pantry led into the living room that tripled as the bedroom and dining room. A small kitchen and bathroom completed the apartment. Boxy, wooden cabinets reached to the tall ceiling, holding books, a television set, stereo, and clothes.

Boris staggered around, knocking into the chairs, trying to be a graceful host. I had difficulty understanding much of what he rambled on about. Slurred Russian was impossible for me.

"*Eta maya zhena*." Boris flapped a color photograph of his wife in front of me. The print was faded, but I could make out the pleasant face of a young woman in a straight dress, standing in a park. I thanked Boris for showing me the photo. He hurried across the room and fished out a ten-inch stack of photographs from a drawer. I suddenly felt very tired. I looked at a dozen of the photos before giving up.

"*Spasiba.*" I told Boris thank you but that I had to go. I stood up.

"*Nyet, Zhon!*" He grabbed at me, laughing, and insisting that I be his overnight guest.

I moved toward the door, but he held onto me. I tried to explain that I had to go back to the hotel. I was supposed to get up in less than three hours to catch the train. Boris nodded eagerly, then ran to the icebox and came back with a withered apple the size of a small plum. I thanked him and put it in my pocket. When I got to the door, Boris leaped in front of me and latched it shut with a hook. Then he grabbed me around the shoulders, laughing, insisting I stay the night.

My humor began to wear thin. He was obsessively interested that I be his guest for the night. Was he hitting on me? Or maybe he collected tourists in his freezer. My thread of hope was that he did have a wife and some very nice friends.

Boris didn't release his grip. I wanted to get out of there. We waltzed around the living room awkwardly until I pried him off. I went for the door and knocked the latch open.

Boris grabbed me from behind pinning my arms as I dragged him a few steps outside. I was starting to get more desperate. Russian hospitality had me in a bearhug at two o'clock in the morning in a dark alley in Siberia.

No matter what I said, he wouldn't let me go. I thought he'd finally relent. But he was just playing with me, laughing himself into oblivion. My humor was gone. Textbook unpleasantries weren't working. "Boris, I must go now." "Boris, this does not appeal to me." And "I am not happy with this situation, Boris."

I wanted to say, "Hey, gorilla breath, get your frigging meat hooks off me or I'll give ya one in the eye!" I thought I'd have to punch my way out of his grip, although making him angry seemed a bad idea. He wasn't acting mean at all. He seemed to think he was being playful, even though obsessive.

Okay," I said, "I'll be your guest." I turned to walk back toward the open door. Boris was pleased. He dropped his grip and told me how happy he was. Now or never. I took off down the dark alley. I could hear heavy footsteps after me. "*Zhon! Zhon!*"

I hit the street and broke into a sprint under dark overhanging trees. Behind me I heard Boris's forlorn voice echoing through the streets as he fell behind me. "*Zhon! Zhon!*" He sounded hurt and sad. Maybe even lonely. But I kept running.

A Long Way to Perm

A young boy huddled under a blanket in the opposite bunk aboard the Trans-Siberian Express. He held both legs tightly against his chest and stared at me. I sat up shaking my head. He'd boarded the train while I was asleep.

"*Dobray ootrum,*" I said.

He responded quietly to my sleepy greeting but looked worried. I glanced at my watch. I'd slept about three hours since a pre-dawn departure from Irkutsk Station. I flopped back down on my pillow and stared up at the laminate bottom of the upper bunk.

I had been dreaming about an enormous, winged dragon with crimson eyes and shimmering scales rising out of the Pacific Ocean. The creature pursued me in a nightmarish chase. I had been so relieved to wake and find myself safely in the middle of Siberia. The rhythm of the rails soothed my nerves. I wondered if I'd thrashed around or called out while fleeing the nightmare.

I looked over at the boy again. He looked quickly away and focused his attention out the window as we rolled to a stop at Cheremkhova Station.

As the morning progressed, I managed to pry a little information out of my reluctant, fourteen-year-old roommate. He was Erik from the city of Usolye-Sibirskoye, along the Angara River. His mother and father had sent him off to visit his grandparents for a couple of weeks of summer vacation. The grandparents lived in Western Siberia near the city of Tomsk, nine hundred miles down the tracks.

I pulled out my Russian Scrabble board and set it up on the table between us. The checkered game board and small, wooden, Cyrillic tiles quickly absorbed his interest. I simplified the rules, and it took just a few turns for Erik to master the concept of intersected spellings and double-point scores. Then he stomped me three games in a row. With his new confidence, Erik relaxed and became more talkative. We shared a glass of tea.

"Erik," I asked, "may I buy you lunch in the dining car?" He looked down at a sack on the floor, then back at me with a shy expression.

"*Nyet, spasiba.*" He thanked me but said his mother had made him a lot of food for the trip. I left unescorted for the restaurant car.

When I returned to the cabin after lunch, Erik sat up expectantly and smiled. He closed his book. I noticed a picture of a dog on the cover.

"Do you want to play the game?" His anxious expression made me chuckle. He'd waited politely until I looked settled before asking me. I set up the Cyrillic Scrabble board. Erik turned all the wooden tiles face down with his long slender fingers and eagerly selected a dozen characters. He had expressive, dark eyes, and his face looked almost like porcelain. His lower lip always stuck out a little.

The train creaked to a stop in the small town of Zima. I recognized the name of this tiny Siberian hamlet located near the childhood home of Yevgeny Yevtushenko, the Russian poet. It was no different than any of the other small station stops I'd seen, but Yevtushenko's writings had given me a glimpse of life here.

Barefoot boys at the fishing hole with pockets full of bread. Uncle Andrei smelling of petrol and virgin forest, carrying the children on his shoulders. Farmhouses, barns, and local bureaucrats. The same images that permeate rural America. I wondered if Erik had a favorite fishing hole.

We played Scrabble for another three hours while the train raced west across Siberia. Erik was a good teacher. He corrected my misspellings and taught me new words. I never did beat him. After four trouncings, I called for a break. Erik sat still for a moment, then pulled out a satchel of papers. He placed a photograph proudly on the table. It was a black and white portrait of a Collie.

Jake

"That's my dog."

I picked it up and nodded approvingly. "What's his name?"

"Jake."

I wasn't ready for that. Maybe Fidovich or Comrade Spike, but Jake? I was supposed to be in Russia, and here is this kid telling me his name is Erik and he's got a dog named Jake.

I pulled out a photograph of my own. "That's my dog," I countered, "named Pyos." *Pyos* meant watchdog in Russian.

"A Russian name?" he inquired with slight disbelief. He held the photo close and studied it. I didn't realize it then, but I was sitting next to a pint-sized dog expert.

Erik emptied his entire satchel of photographs and books onto the table. He was studying at a dog training school. He knew dogs inside out, judging from the detailed charts of canine muscle structures and a book on the psychology of training and control. Erik hopped over to my bunk and sat next to me to show his photo collection. Scores of German Shepherds and Rottweilers were being put through their paces at a Siberian dog institute.

"That's me," Erik pointed at a little guy wearing an oversized padded dog-attack suit with extra-long, quilted arms. It transformed him into a stuffed scarecrow with a pea for a head. Another photo caught an attacking dog in midair, fangs bared, a second before contact.

While Erik and I traded dog stories, the Trans-Siberian Express whisked through taiga forest, across open meadow, and past village after village. We stopped at several small towns like Zima.

Erik noticed my fascination with the towns dotting the countryside. He dug through his cardboard suitcase and handed me a paperback guide. It was a station-by-station account of the entire rail journey from Vladivostok to Moscow, including some of the remote spurs that crossed into northern Siberia. Erik showed me Taiga Station. He would meet a local train there to the city of Tomsk, where his grandparents lived. I thumbed ahead to see what the tracks had in store after Novosibirsk, but the pages were chewed in half and ripped out.

"Jake did that," Erik said, grinning. The city of Sverdlovsk and all of its railways lay in ruins, teeth marks everywhere.

He dug further into his travel supplies and pulled out a couple of plastic bags of food and a deck of playing cards.

"You want to play a game?" He held up the cards and spread out an offering of his mom's homemade cookies and garden carrots. "An American game," he suggested.

What, Rummy? Hearts? Poker? Yeah, poker, we'll play for your cookies. They all seemed too complicated. Something simple. The game War came to mind. But I hesitated to tell Erik the name. *Voynu*, "war" to Russians, conjured an image of horror, not of games.

"I know a game." I improvised a new title: "*Shastleevway.*"

Good Fortune. Erik learned fast. We each won a couple of hands.

After the games, I gave Erik a photograph of my dog and her puppies, and he gave me a photo of a young Rottweiler he'd trained since it was a puppy.

Then I gave him three postcards from Humboldt County. One was of the commercial fishing fleet tied up in the bay at sunset, another of two people standing next to a giant redwood. The picture of the big tree brought a look of amazement to Erik's face, but it was the third card that stunned him. It was one of those joke postcards showing a huge rainbow trout lashed across the bed of a five-ton truck, a happy fisherman at the wheel. Erik stared at the card. He glanced up at me a couple of times but held onto the card with both hands.

"*Eta shootka*," I said. That's a joke. I thought I'd better qualify the trick photograph. He laughed and shook his head.

"This is joke also?" He confidently held up the postcard of giant redwoods and tiny people.

"No, that's real," I said.

Erik looked uncertain as he glanced back and forth between the two cards before adding them to his satchel. He thanked me again and said that he'd put them up over his bed when he got home. A few moments later, he carefully removed a photograph from his collection.

"This is a present, too." His long fingers held the black and white glossy portrait of Jake.

When I got back to the cabin after dinner that evening, a middle-aged man and his daughter had taken the two extra bunks in our compartment. Erik smiled a little, but he seemed reserved. The young girl was lying quietly on her upper bunk. I exchanged a greeting with her father, who was wearing an old threadbare suit that had probably been stylish in Stalin's era. His leathery face accented his fierce eyes. Erik seemed intimidated by this deep-voiced, gruff man.

The man pulled out a bottle of vodka and snapped a finger to his throat. I joined him in a shot. He handed me a chunk of bread as a chaser. We talked a little, but his conversation became interrogative.

"How much does this cost?" he asked, roughly fingering my warm-up suit. "Which is better, U.S. or USSR?"

I had just endured a lengthy bout of dialogue with a young Soviet fellow in the dining car, and I didn't have the energy for another exchange. I shrugged my shoulders.

"How much money do you make in work? How much does it cost to travel in Soviet Union?" The old man questioned me sharply. He seemed a little resentful. His hands looked coarse from hard physical labor. I was young. I had the time, money, and mobility to travel across Siberia.

Sergei — we shared a dining table one evening on the Trans-Siberian Express

His daughter murmured from the upper bunk, "No, Papa, no politics." He told her to hush and pressed on with his sharp enquiries.

Early the next morning, the train rolled to a halt at Mariinsk Station, where the man and his daughter would get off. He put his hand on my shoulder and offered me some morning bread. He seemed conciliatory. I think he'd been a little drunk the night before. We tossed back another shot of vodka before he left the cabin.

Erik and I traded addresses over morning tea. He got off at Taiga Station. We waved to each other as the train pulled out. He looked small standing all alone in front of the station with that lower lip stuck out and his cardboard suitcase full of dog books.

A cool mist fell over Novosibirsk, Siberia's largest city. The railway station teemed with hundreds of travelers. Announcements boomed from a loudspeaker high overhead, flooding the station with echoes of train destinations, platform numbers, and departure times.

Outside, bass rumblings of diesel-electric locomotives vibrated the air as several trains idled at the station. A uniformed porter driving a luggage jitney cursed and beeped his way through the throng of travelers.

"*Papa! Papa!*" A young woman's voice cried out. A slight figure in a white dress ran the length of the platform, clutching several packages in her hands.

"*Papa!*" Tears streamed from her eyes. An aged man emerged from a small crowd across the platform. He threw his arms open and hugged her with joy.

"*Papa! Ya shlah nepravlna platforma,*" she cried, hugging him around the neck. She had gone to the wrong platform. They separated and admired each other for a moment. Her young, rounded features contrasted with his toothless, gaunt, unshaven face. Tears rolled down his cheeks, too. She handed him a bag of food and a small parcel.

The conductor's yellow flag dropped. She threw her arms around his neck again. He kissed her cheeks, shuffled into his car and a moment later, his head emerged from an open window. He reached out to touch hands with her as his train slowly began to roll.

The smell of diesel smoke and wet asphalt lingered in the mist. A wash of sunlight pierced the western clouds, transforming gray mists into subtle gold. The young woman in the white dress waved as her father's train disappeared out of Novosibirsk Station.

After nearly a week of riding the rails westward, twenty-four hours a day, across Siberia, I began to suspect that Moscow was a mythical city, which people talked about but never reached.

An abandoned Orthodox church with onion domes rested in a green meadow on the far side of a river. It was surely the same church I'd seen the first day aboard the train in the Soviet Far East. The Trans-Siberian Express was someone's cruel joke, an endless loop of track.

I was doomed to ride the rails eternally, a modern incarnation of the Flying Dutchman. It had seemed so innocent at first, all those travelers coming and going: Pavel, Erik, the Austrian, and the Japanese climber. They had all gotten off somewhere. I was still aboard. And now at Novosibirsk someone new had entered my cabin: a woman and her son. They didn't know my fate.

Abandoned church along the Trans-Siberian Express rail line

We started the day by partially ignoring each other after exchanging pleasantries. Tanya appeared to be in her twenties, and Alek was her 220-volt, five-year-old son. They were traveling to the city of Perm on the western slope of the Ural Mountains. Tanya was quiet and reclusive, staring out the window a lot.

Following our afternoon tea break, Alek rounded up the remaining sugar cubes, each with a speeding train illustrated on its blue paper wrapper, and blatantly devoured them. Then he bounced on the bed and made wild animal sounds for some agonizing minutes.

"How far is Perm?" I asked.

"We'll arrive tomorrow morning," Tanya answered, abandoning her out-of-body experience. She attempted to quiet Alek, but he kept fidgeting, then ran out the door and down the corridor. I wondered if Tanya had ever heard about the connection between sugar and childhood behavior.

Alek returned shortly, transforming the rhythmic quiet of the train compartment into a squeal fest. He'd brought two small friends in to play—a cute little girl in a yellow dress with ribbons in her blond curls and tiny red shoes and her older brother, less impressive with his snot-stained shirt and loud, sharp laughter. He egged Alek on to new heights—the upper bunk.

I'm not sure what got to Tanya first, the continual sprawl of the Barabinskaya Steppe or Alek. He'd climbed to the top bunk, dangled, screamed, and hit the floor a dozen times. With measured calm, Tanya ushered the other children out the door to their quarters. When she returned, she instructed Alek to lie down. He obeyed. All was momentarily quiet in the Western Basin of Siberia.

I read for a while, then drifted off into a nap. Sudden bursts of shellfire woke me. Alek blasted something out of the air with an umbrella. I found refuge in the dining car over a bowl of soup. We pulled into Barabinsk Station. Perm was still eight or nine hundred miles west.

When I returned to the cabin, Tanya looked up from a book.

"*Teakah*." She put a finger to her lips, accenting the word "quiet," then pointed to the overhead bunk. Alek was sound asleep.

After some silence, Tanya said that Alek became hyperactive whenever they traveled. They were coming from her mother's house in Alma Ata, Kazakhstan, after a two-week summer visit.

We tried to play Russian Scrabble, but the game progressed slowly. Tanya looked out the window between turns. It helped me that she was a daydreamer. I spelled *beriozka*, a twenty-seven-point word meaning birch tree.

Near the end of the game, Alek woke up. He hung his head over the bunk and smiled at me. I began to like him. He got up and played quietly on the floor with a green dump truck. I was just about to win the Scrabble game when Alek backed his ten-wheel Kamaz rig up to the Scrabble board and began loading it up with the wooden Cyrillics. Tanya didn't protest. I watched my twenty-seven-point word drop into the truck, along with most of the other tiles.

Alek drove off, out the door and down the corridor. I looked over at Tanya, thinking she'd stop him, but she just sat there. I imagined Alek dumping the truckload of Cyrillics into the toilet and flushing them onto the tracks of Siberia. The thought of the bathroom made me queasy. Since leaving Irkutsk, its condition had gradually deteriorated. Everything was always wet, and a thin slime of muddy footprints had accumulated on the floor.

I caught up with Alek halfway down the carpeted corridor. He was crawling along on his hands and knees between people's feet being a diesel truck.

"Alek," I said gingerly, catching him by the seat of the pants, hoping he wouldn't scream when I took the tiles back. Alek giggled when he saw me. I was the big dumb guy who couldn't speak Russian very well.

I pointed at his dump truck load. "It's not possible for this game to go from our train room."

He laughed and chattered back at me in Russian. He sounded like an animated chipmunk, but he drove his dump truck back to the cabin.

After a brief station stop at Tatarsk, our wagon hostess brought the evening tea. Alek sat on his mother's lap and scooped up a few of the sugar cubes, then moved to a corner of the bunk to indulge in frantic nibbling.

"Do you want to eat?" Tanya asked me. I refused politely, but noticed mineral water, fruit, bread, and cookies in her food bag. There was a chicken in there, too. I accepted the invitation for a homegrown, homemade dinner. We ordered more tea.

After the meal, Alek curled up next to Tanya and watched the flash of landscape pass by the cabin window. He grinned at me once. His smile had definite charm after a few moments of quiet. I think he liked me.

"Tanya," I asked, "is talking with me like speaking with a five-year-old child?"

"No, not a five-year-old," she answered, rolling her eyes to the ceiling and back, as if the answer were written up there. She was sparing me the laughter. "Mmmm, maybe a four-year-old."

"Oh."

Near midnight, the Trans-Siberian Express pulled into Omsk Station. Alek was sound asleep in the upper bunk, lying on his back with his mouth open, probably dreaming about forests of sugar cane.

Tanya asked if I wanted to go for a walk together. A surprising number of people were gathered outside Omsk Station for such a late evening. Young couples, elderly people, travelers, and a few off-duty soldiers walked along the concrete platforms in the warm night air. The crowd was oddly silent. Some people ate ice cream bars purchased from a vendor. Others sat idly on benches beneath trees. We bought some ice cream and joined the quiet procession along the station platform.

Suddenly, a perfectly folded paper airplane glided out of a first-class cabin window. Another followed. Then another. Two Asian men wearing glasses peered out the window, laughing. A transformation took place.

An old man wearing a baggy suit stooped and picked up one of the paper airplanes. He threw it with the fascination of a young boy. A heavyset, older woman picked it up and threw it again, laughing out loud. Others joined in. In a moment's time, half a dozen paper airplanes sailed through the air. Children, teenagers, and older people scampered and hobbled for a chance to throw a small airborne paper creation. Giggles and laughter bubbled from the crowd at Omsk Station.

Tanya pointed up at the stars. "Do you know that one? *Eta bolshoi myedvyed.*" She identified it as the Big Bear.

"In America, we call it the Big Dipper."

I moved away from the lights for a better view of the stars. In the middle of Siberia, the same celestial images twinkled overhead as in America. Discovering Big Bear made me feel closer to home.

At seven o'clock the next morning, a grinding noise woke me. Alek, chewing up a stash of sugar cubes, smiled and tapped on the walls.

Outside, the city of Sverdlovsk rose into view. This was where the Tsar and his family had disappeared from the world. Perhaps Siberia had swallowed them, too. As we whooshed into the station, I saw a man without a nose waiting for a train.

After Sverdlovsk, we lost the Big Sky. The Trans-Siberian Express ascended into the ancient Ural Mountains, divider of the European and Asian continents. The terrain changed from sprawling steppe and clumped deciduous forests to pine-covered mountains. The air cooled as we climbed. Ural rivers moved more swiftly than the meandering lowland waters.

The Ural Mountains had been chiseled by time into a low, rounded range like the Appalachians. Small village homes lined the upper banks of a wide, green river that descended westward into European Russia.

Many of the homes were painted blue or yellow, with ornate white wooden window frames and roof trim. They stood like ornaments against the mountain greenery. The Trans-Siberian Express gained speed descending into Europe. Perm would be the first major station west of the Urals.

A strong smell interrupted my reverie of continental transformation. I'd forgotten about Alek. He'd been into Tanya's purse and was emptying a bottle of perfume onto his head.

"Alek!" Tanya grabbed the container and scolded him, her voice trailing off in frustration. Alek rubbed his hair and quickly wiped his scented mitts across his shirt. The whole cabin reeked. Diesel fumes couldn't have been worse. I opened the window.

Tanya asked me if I'd watch Alek while she went down the hall to the tiny metal bathroom.

Alek and me alone? I cringed at the thought. What if he threw a tantrum? What if he wouldn't mind me? He could jabber circles around my Russian.

"Sure, no problem," I lied. Tanya looked at me for a moment.

"You want to do this, yes? I'll only be a few minutes."

All I had to do was make sure he didn't hurt himself or escape out the door. I remembered the pillow and bedding compartment under the bunk. Maybe I could coax him to climb in. I could shut the lid and sit on it until she returned.

"Sure, it's all right." Tanya left with her travel bag, and I felt like a watch dog on duty.

Alek sat across from me grinning, his legs sticking out straight on the bunk. He looked innocent enough. After another cube, he shredded the back page of Pravda, a Soviet newspaper and blew spit all over his mother's bed.

"Alek," I cautioned, "*Tavaya mot etova nenravitsa.*" He grinned at my warning that his mother would not like this, then spit on the table and pasted the shredded bits of Pravda on the tabletop. He was kind of cute, in a way.

About fifteen minutes later, Tanya returned with her hair brushed neatly, wearing a fresh summer dress and makeup. "How was he?"

"He was a good boy," I replied, "but there's a little problem on the table there." I pointed at the bubbly saliva pool of shredded paper.

"Oh, Alek! I will tell your father." She mopped up the soggy Pravda creation with a hand towel. Alek got very quiet.

At Perm, Tanya's husband greeted her and Alek with flowers and kisses. I walked along the rail platform looking at all the car windows. Nearly two hundred windows framed the cabins on each side of the elongated train, each one like a portrait: an old country *babushka* in a flowered scarf; tiny children pressing their fingers and faces against the glass like frogs; a military officer with three gold insignias across his shoulder and a scowl on his face; a young couple with Soviet champagne on their table.

As the Trans-Siberian Express again moved westward, the Urals diminished in the distance. I returned to my room to find a Ukrainian railway worker had moved in. We would share the compartment for a day and a night. And there would be others, too, a young woman from Kirov, and another from Murmansk. Every day for a week, twenty-four hours a day, Trans-Siberian passengers lived in tiny cubicles, hurtling along steel rails on an ocean-sized land mass. Behind us lay nearly five thousand miles of Siberian Asia. Our train raced into Russia's heartland. We'd finally made it to Perm, but Moscow was still very much a myth, nearly nine hundred miles to the west.

The Golden Ring

When I crossed the border into the Soviet Union, I had one name and a hand-scrawled phone number on a piece of paper in my pocket. One phone number, out of a country of 275 million people. An older couple in my Russian language class at our local university had passed it along to me. They'd spent a two-week vacation in Sochi, Russia, on the Black Sea coast and taken their daughter with them. Their daughter had met a young Moscow woman on the boardwalk, and they'd spent several days together seeing the sights and establishing a friendship. Layla spoke English, they said. Phone numbers were exchanged. I was handed a small, handwritten piece of paper: Layla 095-724-3785.

When the Trans-Siberian Express finally rolled into Moscow's Yaroslavsky Station, after nearly two weeks of traversing epic landscapes and making periodic stops at provincial Siberian cities, I was overwhelmed by the magnitude and historic character of Moscow. It was like stepping out of a time machine. The Soviet mega-city shocked me—streets wide enough to land jumbo jets, pedestrians striding at a New York City pace, subway stations that looked like fine arts museums, immense sprawling buildings as far as the eye could see, and at the epicenter stood the Kremlin. Black Soviet limousines—Volgas, Chaikas, and

Moscow neighborhood street

ZiLs—popped in and out of the Kremlin's Spasskaya Tower entrance on Red Square, carrying military men and bureaucrats.

I had planned to call Layla, but I felt a little intimidated to just jump off the train and make the call, so I waited.

For three days, I wandered out of my hotel every morning at sunrise and walked Moscow streets until late at night. The city of almost nine million didn't seem threatening at all. Women walked alone in the city center after midnight. There were no bars. No street hoodlums. Crime didn't seem to exist, at least from what I could see. I contrasted this to my time in New York City two years before, when street crimes were at a historic high.

I did all the obvious sightseeing—Red Square, St. Basil's, the Kremlin, GUM, Tretyakov, the Moscow Metro, Gorky Park—then I eventually worked my way to outlying neighborhoods and districts.

One morning, I exited Kolomenskoye Metro Station with no plan and just started walking. That's how I discovered Kolomenskoye Park, a sprawling outdoor museum with nine hundred acres of trees and fields, its history dating back to the 1300s. Tsar Alexis I built an elaborate and ornate, 250-room, summer palace on the grounds, where Peter the Great spent some of his childhood days.

Kolomenskoye was a mesmerizing blend of ancient architecture with its sixteenth century Church of the Ascension spire and stone structures that looked out over the Moscow River and the city center in the distance. It felt like a refuge.

That evening, after spending all day at Kolomenskoye, I called Layla from a telephone booth by the metro. It was time to reach out.

The phone rang. It was my first phone call in the USSR.

"*Allo, slewshiyou,*" a woman's voice said. Hello, I'm listening.

"Is this Layla?" I asked.

"Yes."

I explained how I came to have her number. She said it was fortunate that I had called, because tomorrow she would be moving to another apartment and this number would be disconnected. She suggested we meet that evening.

Layla was a university graduate with an extensive network of connections, I would soon learn. She was Russian, a Moscovite, but of Asian-Korean descent from the Soviet Far East. Her English was excellent, and we seldom said a word in Russian, which seemed like a conversation freeway after two weeks struggling through primary Russian language connections. We met three times during my days in Moscow. Each time she introduced me to new people.

Moscow Landmarks – The Kremlin and Church of the Ascension at Kolomenskoye

I was invited to a dinner party and then to meet three of her university friends. All three young men spoke English well. Sasha was an engineer who had been studying the environmental health impacts of the Aral Sea drying up in Central Asia because of irrigation diversions. As the large lake retreated, it exposed deposits of agricultural chemicals that dried and blew in the winds. People were breathing those chemicals.

The other Sasha was a medical doctor who had an interest in black market developments and currency, and he seemed naturally entrepreneurial. He was curious, and I could see his mind turning over my responses, trying to see if there was an angle to pursue, or not.

The third, Alex, was hard to pin down, but he knew the underground music scene, especially in Leningrad. While the two Sashas were intense and highly focused, Alex was naturally casual. He had an excellent command of American slang and unruly blond hair. He might have passed for a surfer in Santa Monica.

Layla; Maxim, a talented keyboardist in the alternative music scene, and his wife

A Moscow dinner party

Layla tended to sit back and just see where the conversations would go. She didn't interject herself that much socially, even though she seemed to know a lot of people. When Alex found out I was going to rent a car and drive to Leningrad, he offered to get me tickets to an underground concert in that city.

On my last day in Moscow, I returned to Kolomenskoye. I found it a place of solitude and inspiration. I could walk the open fields and look out over the city to the north, while taking in the grandeur of the old churches. The place seemed to defy time. It was the preservation of a long-ago era in Russia's history, before the modern world.

And I was about to go deeper into it.

I was scheduled to pick up a rental car the next morning and begin a two-week road trip into the Golden Ring of Russia, a string of small provincial towns and cities to the northeast of Moscow that contained the ancient churches and monasteries of Eastern Orthodox tradition that survived the thirteenth century Mongol invasion. I would be driving to historic places that I'd read about, such as Vladimir, Suzdal, Zagorsk, Ivanova, and Yaroslavl, towns and cities that had just lived on pages of books and in my mind. But, tomorrow, they would start to come alive as I drove into the Golden Ring.

A traffic policeman waved his black and white baton at my Soviet rental car, and I stopped. I was on the eastern outskirts of Moscow, on Gorky Highway. Brilliant gold foreign license plates made the car easy to spot. Soviets had black and white plates. I knew I'd overshot the traffic tower by a hundred feet. I watched the officer—dressed in a long, gray military coat, an officer's hat, and leather boots—approach in the side view mirror.

This was my second police stop in my attempt to find a road out of Moscow. When I got my car early in the morning, I'd driven north from the city for over an hour and then spontaneously taken a small country road in an easterly direction that I thought would take me toward Ivanova and Suzdal. There were no highway signs. It was just a hunch. The road cut through rolling fields and birch tree forests. But a policeman had stopped me at the first traffic tower I encountered.

"You can't proceed on this road," that officer had said, wagging his finger at me. He smiled and pointed me back south, gesturing beyond the birch forest, toward Southern Russia or the Indian Ocean, somewhere far over the horizon. Okay, that wasn't so bad, as traffic stops go, I thought.

Moscow freeway in 1984

I eventually found Gorky Highway. But now I was stopped again at another traffic control tower, and this policeman wasn't smiling.

"*Zdrastvweetye?*" Where are you driving?

"*Suzdal.*"

"From what country are you?" The policeman fixed unblinking eyes on me and leveled quick questions. His brusque manner was difficult for me to interpret. He became visibly irritated that I was headed into the countryside and couldn't answer his questions.

"Give me your passport. Your travel visa. All your documents!"

Gulp.

I handed him everything, the motel and camping vouchers, rail tickets, airplane tickets, my international driver's license, my whole identity. He disappeared inside the two-story glass control tower. All of a sudden, the Soviet State seemed ominous. I wondered if the policeman could just walk into his tower, punch a few buttons and know if I should be sitting there at that moment.

While he was inside the control tower, my mind raced as I sat on the roadside thinking back on how the day had begun, when I picked up my rental car. I recalled how the friendly Intourist agent chatted away about the terms of the rental and then proudly revealed the compact, stick-shift Zhiguli that I would be driving for the next two weeks. He explained that the car was built by a joint venture between USSR's AvtoVAZ and Italy's Fiat. It had a reputation for having a great heater. Getting the car hadn't been a problem, just a few signatures and an American passport. The agent smiled and held the keys out to me.

"Have a very good time. We will see you in two weeks."

"What about a map?"

"I'm sorry," he apologized, "but there are no highway maps."

"Where can I get one?" I asked.

"Nowhere." He looked at me blankly.

I drove to a nearby Soviet bookstore and a department store. But they had no maps and had no idea where somebody would find a map. I could probably get a map of the German invasion of 1941 or Napoleon's retreat in 1812, but I couldn't buy a 1984 highway map in Moscow.

I drove away in disbelief, nosing the Zhiguli into the rush of traffic, which was sparse compared to urban America's traffic jams. I was going to have to rely on my memory of what the Soviet highway system looked like from the books I had studied at home and where various towns and cities were located.

My itinerary would route me through the Soviet capital several times. All the highways of the region pointed toward Moscow as if it were the ancient hub of a great, spoked wheel. The city itself was circled by five highways that formed a series of rings from the Kremlin out to the suburbs. It had taken me over half the day just to get to the eastern edge of Moscow.

And now here I was.

Footsteps in the gravel. I lurched out of my recollections of the morning and waited for the policeman to deliver the verdict.

With regimented formality, he handed me my papers, offered a military salute, and motioned me forward to Suzdal. I wondered who he called, Intourist or the KGB?

The four-lane highway soon tapered into a narrow, two-way road traversing fields and colorful country villages. Every home had a TV antenna and an outhouse. People carried well water in buckets.

Scores of big trucks rumbled along the asphalt pavement, spewing black smoke out of their stacks and holding back lines of darting passenger cars. The traffic was thick.

I pulled out to pass a tractor-trailer rig. My heart pounded as I accelerated to seventy-five miles per hour. I was in the USSR on the wrong side of the road, flying past a semi with another truck snarling toward me in a cloud of smoke. Everything seemed unpredictable. I slipped back into my lane and slowed down to fifty-five miles per hour, the Soviet speed limit.

After an hour and a half, the road crossed a small river bending through a grove of birch trees where an outdoor grill and picnic area had attracted a crowd of motorists. It looked like an oasis from the two-lane carbon monoxide tube. My orange car added another shade to the M&M collection of red, green, yellow, and brown Soviet compacts parked in the turnout.

Two women in white aprons passively tended the grill in a grassy meadow beside the highway. My taste buds blossomed at the skewers of beef and onion *shashleeks* barbecuing over a bed of hot coals. The older woman in white scraped the skewered meat and onions onto a paper plate and weighed it in grams on a scale. She used an abacus to figure the cost. I bought a bottle of beer and found a vacant table.

Most of the people sitting around were families on summer vacation, or Moscovites with picnic lunches on a country drive. Some broad-shouldered young men arm wrestled with their sleeves rolled up. Their faces and forearms bulged behind locked hands and empty beer pitchers.

After lunch, I sat in the sun and tossed a few pebbles into the river. Some children splashed downstream near a camping area. All the tension from road traffic, policemen, the streets of Moscow, and a train trip without end started to let go. I lay back in the grass and closed my eyes. The highway sounds receded. Summer daydreams settled in against the babbling of children's voices and rush of water.

The road sign pointed north to Suzdal. I was surprised to see a dozen people hitchhiking wearing business suits or dresses. A few carried briefcases. It was five-thirty in the afternoon, on the northern edge of Vladimir, an industrial urban center 120 miles east of Moscow, with a thirteenth century cathedral at its center. It was the first city on my Golden Ring route.

I swerved over and attracted six potential riders.

"Suzdal!" I yelled out the window.

Immediately, all three doors opened, and the car filled with people and briefcases. I pulled away slowly. The small Soviet compact lost its pep with the extra seven hundred pounds aboard.

The city of Vladimir ended abruptly at a row of tall trees lining an irrigation ditch. Across the ditch, farmland spread into the distance.

I scanned all the new faces. They were a cheery group. "Thank God it's Friday" seemed to generate universal relief.

"I speak English very well," a heavily accented voice said from the back seat. Surprised, I glanced in my rearview mirror, then turned for a quick acknowledgement to the man in the middle who spoke. His wide smile supported a pair of thick, dark-rimmed glasses and a small wool sporting cap.

"That's great," I said. "I haven't met many Russians who speak English. Did you study at the university?"

"I speak English very well," he repeated. Everyone in the car snickered.

"Hmmm, I see. So you don't really speak English. You can't understand me. Right?" Another pause.

"Thank you very much," he laughed. "I speak English very well, ha ha ha."

We sailed along at sixty miles an hour surrounded by a sprawling sea of dark-chocolate soil, lush green field crops and a huge blue sky. Two tractors rambled along the horizon. Add a few billboards, and it would look like the American Midwest. The Russian jibber-jabber in the back seat made me feel relaxed, like I was part of a carpool with guys from work.

When I rented the car, I didn't realize that I would be ferrying hitchhikers across Russian highways or that hitchhiking was an acceptable form of Soviet transportation. I'd thumbed across the States a few times, but it seemed different in the USSR. I'd tried it outside of Irkutsk that evening at the bus stop, but nothing had come of it.

My first riders that day had been a young boy and his grandmother. She drew a map to her country home in case I wanted to stop for tea on my way back to Moscow. Then a stocky, middle-aged truck driver climbed into the passenger seat, sporting a Charlie Chaplin moustache and a tweed suit. A small brown felt hat was perched on his head as if it would only be there momentarily.

And now I had a carload of Vladimir-Suzdal commuters. The hitchhiker in the front seat pulled out a one-ruble bill.

"For gasoline."

I tried not to accept the money, but two more rubles came from the back seat.

"I have coupons for gas," I bargained, taking them from my shirt pocket and holding them up for proof. I waved coupons. My passengers waved rubles.

It was four against one. They insisted I take the gas money. "If not for gasoline, then we are buying your dinner for you." End of discussion.

Suzdal broke the northern landscape with a fairytale skyline of old-world Russian architecture. Scores of bulbous onion domes dotted the turreted walls of monasteries and churches. The center dome of Suzdal's kremlin appeared to billow like a midnight-blue hot air balloon drawn to a point. Golden stars and gilded Orthodox crosses adorned the historic crown. The Kamenka River flowed through the town.

I dropped my passengers off in a quaint residential area of ornate wooden homes and narrow streets. Only a few thousand people lived in Suzdal. When the comedian got out, he bent over and looked back inside the car with a grin on his face. "Thank you very much. I speak English very well. Goodbye."

Two Moscow travelers I met at a cafe; they showed me around Suzdal

Androv threw another log in the fire, then prodded it with a length of steel pipe. Orange sparks swarmed into the early morning darkness at Suzdal. We stared into the flames, listening to the crickets and bull frogs celebrate a full moon over the Kamenka River. Nightingales warbled from a nearby wooded area, first one, then another, their songs echoing across the small valley and into Suzdal.

Suzdal is one of the oldest towns in Russia, dating back almost one thousand years, to a time before Moscow was even imagined. The small town is crowned with dozens of Orthodox churches, built during the thirteenth to nineteenth centuries. The churches stood out with their colorful blue onion domes dotted with gold stars, green domes, black domes, and white stone spires. Most of the churches were either closed, boarded up, or served as historical museums rather than places of worship.

Suzdal landscape along the Kamenka River

Our campfire blazed on a knoll above the river, near the towering white brick walls and eight-story turrets of the former Spaso-Yevfimiev Monastery. Tule fog hung around the silent, sixteenth-century structure. Androv opened his canvas rucksack, took out a dozen potatoes and buried them carefully in the coals at the edge of the fire.

"These will be good," he said.

"Who wants to swim?" Sasha spoke out across the fire. Androv shook his head no. I didn't want to jump in the river, either. It was three o'clock in the morning, and we'd been sitting around the fire since midnight.

Sasha, a young construction worker from the city of Ulyanovsk, jumped up and expanded his chest. "I'm going into the water." He flexed his arms, unfastened the row of tiny plastic buttons on his shirt, then trotted off to the river. A few minutes later I heard a loud splash and a few yelps.

The river was partially hidden by the mist that hugged the lower meadow. I could hear Sasha swimming but couldn't see him except for an occasional luminescent dash of water.

Earlier that evening, I had walked down to the river hoping to hear the nightingales after having had a late dinner in a restaurant. The moonlight made it easy to see the dirt path that wound along the banks of the Kamenka River. That's how I met Androv. He had appeared out of the fog, walking across a wooden footbridge, and invited me to join him and his friend Sasha around a fire he'd built on the hillside near the monastery.

"How many people are there in the city where you live?" Androv asked, looking curiously over the flame toward me. The two of us had spoken very little that night. He seemed a quiet man, staring into the fire for long periods with a distant look in his eyes. His bearded profile disguised his youth, and by the firelight, I kept seeing him as a Viking.

"Hmm, about four hundred people."

"Four hundred thousand?" He thought I'd left out a word.

"*Nyet, tolka chetearista.*" No, only four hundred.

"*Eta mala goradoak.*" A very small town. Androv lived in Suzdal. He understood the life of small towns.

"In my town," I pointed to the fire, "my friends and I make fires on the beach at the Pacific Ocean and sit together until late at night."

"Yes, here in the countryside, we do that, too." Androv said.

I glanced from the crackling flame to the northern constellations. Nightingale songs echoed around the silhouetted monastery towering above us. The ancient stone walls and onion domes had sprouted in the aftermath of Genghis Khan's horseback warriors and the Mongols' two-hundred-year occupation of Russia. The churches and monasteries of Suzdal were now government preserves of art and history.

I tried to tell Androv I was glad to be sitting by a fire with Russians, along a tributary of the Volga River, surrounded by architecture reflecting a thousand years of culture. Androv listened and nodded his head.

"We have a very long history."

I thought about my family—sailing out of the North Sea three hundred years before, bound for the new world. Ten generations in America seemed young compared to the Russian millennium.

Androv tossed more wood on the fire. The sudden flare of heat felt good against the early morning chill. A cluster of small, wooden roofs peeped through the mist on the far bank of the Kamenka. Earlier that night I had walked among newly constructed buildings that were part of a film set. Piles of lumber scraps littered the narrow walkways and fog drifted among dwellings. Androv had been the watchman.

A movie was being filmed by Soviet, Italian, and American producers about Peter The Great, the six-foot-eight tsar who forged Russia into a world power at the turn of the seventeenth century.

"Listen," Androv paused. A dog howled a long mournful cry. "Sabaka sings to the moon."

Sasha hustled back to the fire, shivering, wearing only his trousers. Androv looked over at him, amused.

"Androv," Sasha chattered. "How much time before potatoes?"

"Maybe half an hour," Androv replied slowly, glancing at the coals.

"*Xarasho.*" Sasha took his metal wristwatch from his pocket, flexing his arms and chest. His mannerisms reminded me of a fellow I'd run a jackhammer with one summer working highway construction out in Utah.

After the flames died down, Androv reached into the coals with a stick and flipped a potato onto an open newspaper he'd prepared, then cut into the blackened skin.

"They're ready."

One at a time, Androv uncovered the charred potatoes and pulled them from the fire. He emptied a bag of brown bread and cucumbers onto the newspaper, arranging the food in separate piles.

Sasha had disappeared for about fifteen minutes and now had returned with a bottle of vodka. It seemed that in every town in Russia you could get a bottle of vodka at any hour. Even in a sleepy little country town like Suzdal.

Sasha threw more wood on the fire.

"*Vodka, xocheesh?*" he offered. We picked away at the food and passed the bottle around until it was empty.

We idled the time away into the early morning hours. At one point, Sasha sat up and asked me if I liked jokes.

"I don't know," I said, "Try one." I'd had problems understanding Soviet jokes because punch lines were lined with inside understandings of how things worked, and the ironies were lost on me. Not this one, though. Sasha began.

A man is sitting on a hill eating lunch in the Ural Mountains. He sees two workers with shovels walk across the fields below him. They both stop, one digs a hole, then they wait five minutes. The second man fills in the hole, tamping it gently. They walk another ten paces and repeat the sequence. This goes on for an hour or so until a dozen neatly lined up holes dot the field. The man on the hill is miffed.

"*Shto bweevaeyet?*" What is happening? The man walks down into the field, approaches the two workers as they pause between diggings and asks, pointing to all the holes, "*Shto vwee delitye?*" What are you doing? One worker leaning on a shovel replies, "We're a three-man tree-planting crew, but the one who plants the tree didn't come to work today."

The sun would be up in a couple hours. I stretched out alongside the fire on a patch of grass and leaned back against a small log round. Sasha and Anton spoke quietly by the fireside. The moon dipped low on the horizon, then vanished from sight.

As the eastern sky lightened, I bid good day to the two men, and walked down the hillside, following the dirt path. The Kamenka still lay partially hidden beneath ground fog. I looked back to the distant hillside and the long white rampart of the monastery. A faint waft of smoke rose pale in the morning light. Androv and Sasha were barely visible, sitting on log rounds near the embers. The nightingales and crickets weren't singing anymore. But the bullfrogs welcomed a new day.

A string of oncoming motorists flashed their headlights as a warning. I was cruising about twenty miles an hour over the posted speed limit. So were most of the other drivers. My foot came off the gas instantly, and I entered the speed trap.

A Soviet motorcycle policeman sat behind a bus stop shelter holding a metal radar device that looked like a vaporizer. He studied the readout, not noticing my foreign plates as I zoomed past.

The first few days on Soviet highways had been strange enough without all the motorists flashing their lights at me. I thought I was doing something wrong. American motorists flash you in the daylight if there's a wreck ahead, but that wasn't the case here.

At one point, I stopped to see if something was visibly wrong with the car.

As I drove on, I noticed that every time lights flashed, I'd then see a traffic cop at the side of the road, either in a compact gold and blue Zhiguli with a red light on the roof or on a green motorcycle. The police always looked ready to go after somebody, but I'd never seen a single ticket being written by the side of the road. I wondered if the patrolman behind the bus stop knew that every motorist on the road knew his proximity. After passing him, I felt confident and started speeding again, flashing my lights at oncoming cars.

I was driving south from Yaroslavl after spending a few days in the Golden Ring region, where fifteenth-century onion-domed churches and monasteries were as common as the Golden Arches at home.

Another provincial village ahead. I slowed to about forty. Scores of brightly painted, little wooden homes stood alongside the tree-lined road. An old brick

church lay in disrepair, surrounded by a yard of farm machinery.

Near the edge of town, a middle-aged woman wearing an apron over a geometric print dress stood at the side of the road and gestured for a ride. I pulled over and stopped under a big shade tree. She hurried over to the car and opened the back door.

"*Zdrastvweetye. Zdrastvweetye.* You are driving to Moscow?" She appeared anxious.

"Yes."

She turned back and motioned to someone. I wondered if this was one of those roadside ploys where a single woman hails a ride, then Uncle Petrov and his four companions with luggage come out from behind a bush.

"Please," the woman turned back to me, "my daughters must go to the train station in Moscow."

"Your daughters?"

Two girls around fourteen years old, dressed like small-town teenagers from a fifties movie and carrying stuffed, vinyl travel bags emerged from the shade.

"*Da.* Is this possible?"

"Of course," I said. I remembered the flat tire in my trunk from the pothole I'd hit that day. Now I was running on the spare. "But I might have to stop." I had forgotten the words for tire and air. The best I could do was a hand charade with an air leak sound, telling her that a soft circle needed repair.

"I understand. That's fine." She nodded and turned to give a hug to each girl. They slipped into the back seat, sticking close together, rolling the window down and giggling. Their mother extended her head through the open window, giving them one last hug and a kiss. "*Shastleevway,*" she said, as she backed away from the car.

I pulled out slowly, being ultra careful so the woman would realize what a safe driver I was and wouldn't worry.

As we left the village, I glanced in my rearview mirror. Both girls waved out the back window. I tried to imagine a mother in her apron on California's

Highway 101, flagging down motorists to take her teenaged daughters into San Francisco so they could catch a train.

"What time does your train leave?"

Shy giggles bubbled from the back seat.

"This evening," one ventured, covering her mouth with her hand.

"*Xarasho.*" No problem. I paused. "Which city are you traveling to?"

"Novgorod. Our aunt and uncle live there." Giggles.

That was about the extent of our conversation.

A country home on the Moscow-Leningrad Highway

A few kilometers down the road, I noticed a blue sign with a monkey wrench on it. I told the girls I had to stop to fix the tire. Two bashful faces nodded.

The repair shop was set back off the road in a grove of trees. About half a dozen cars sat in the parking lot, and a few people milled about. As soon as the shop foreman found out I was a foreigner, my problem became top priority. He took the tire, and I went for a walk. The girls remained in the car.

Outside the office, a gravel path led into a large flower garden with white statues and benches. A lawn with shade trees was a nice place to wait out auto problems.

A portly fellow with lively blue eyes walked up and introduced himself. He'd seen my foreign plates and wanted to know where I was from.

"Who's better, Americans or Russians? Ha, ha, ha. How do you like Soviet Union? As bad as you thought? Ha ha ha."

His chatter bordered on being a one-man show. He asked me questions then quickly filled in the answers with his funny little voice, all the while standing on one foot, then the other. His eyes never strayed from me.

He could have been a standup comedian. But he said he was a physician from the city of Gorky. He and his wife and kids were on a three-week camping trip, driving around in the Golden Ring. He looked more American than I did with his Levis and sandy hair permed into tight little curls. I had on a pair of Russian sandals and a Soviet-made shirt.

"*Vwee znaiyetye Ruskie pisatseyalee?*" he asked, quizzing me on whether I knew Russian writers.

"*Da*. Chekov, Shukshin, and Yevtushenko," I replied.

"*Xarasho*." The man from Gorky nodded, then held out his hand with four fingers proudly extended. He named his favorite American writers, bending each finger down as he spoke, "Mark Tvain, Zhak Loandon, Hemeengvay. You like Faulkner?" he asked.

I'd never read a Faulkner novel, only his short stories. My reply brought a look of astonishment to the physician's round face. "What? You have not read the books of Villiam Faulkner? My friend, you have hole in your education. Ha, ha."

The garage foreman waved me toward the office. A certain form was missing. The bookkeeper fussed through desk drawers, piles of stacked papers, and under boxes, trying to find the right form. Customers came in to ask her questions, but she couldn't help them.

"Oh, Mama!" She slumped back in her chair. "Today is only my second day at this work. Everything is difficult."

She finally came up with the proper form. I signed my name in five places and showed her my passport, visa, and driver's license. The shop had no change, so I got a discount. Ten rubles to repair the tire.

My two riders stood patiently beside the car. The foreman in blue coveralls insisted on rolling the tire out to the car himself and placing it in the trunk. When I pulled out, he and the bookkeeper stood out front and waved goodbye.

By the time we reached Moscow, clouds had darkened the sky. Rain began to fall in sheets. The girls were grumbling about the weather.

I pulled over to get my windshield wipers out of the trunk. Soviet wipers were in short supply. I'd been warned to take them off the car unless it was raining or they'd be stolen.

"Where do you want to go in Moscow?" I asked the girls, after jumping back in out of the rain.

"VDNKH Metro. Do you know where that is?"

It was nearby—a large economic expo center. From there, the underground metro would take them to the train station faster than an automobile, and it only cost a nickel. They both thanked me several times for the ride, then popped open their umbrellas and hurried toward the subway station to continue their journey to Novgorod.

Finding Petrodvorets

If Tamara had only turned on the headlights, I wouldn't have felt so frightened, even though we were hitting over sixty miles an hour in a residential neighborhood at night. The car bottomed out when we bounded across an intersection. I braced one hand against the dashboard. My feet were pressed onto the floorboards.

"What's the matter?" Tamara's voice sounded relaxed, as if we were waiting at a stop light.

"Slow down! You're making me really nervous," I repeated. It had been a real mistake to let this woman drive my car.

Tamara glanced over from behind her wire-rimmed glasses. My stiffened posture with one hand on the dashboard won some sympathy. "But this is how I always drive." She slowed down to fifty-five.

A few minutes later, she turned onto the highway skirting Kalinin, a large city northwest of Moscow near the headwaters of the Volga River. Her speeding didn't bother me so much on the open road. At least Soviet traffic law said headlights could be used on the highway at night. Motorists were supposed to drive with just parking lights in the cities.

"Where are we going?" I asked. This wasn't the way to my campground. She'd offered to drive me across the city so I wouldn't get lost in the winding maze. I was only going to be in Kalinin one night. We certainly weren't going to look at any more war memorials or museums at this hour. Tamara kept both hands on the wheel and watched the road. She didn't talk much while driving.

"I'm taking a different road to your campground. We'll avoid the city. It will be simpler."

I'd met Tamara that afternoon on a park bench along the banks of the Volga River, the longest river in Europe. She walked by and asked me for the time. After staring at my watch for a few seconds, I came up with a somewhat correct Russian response for four-forty. "*Pyat chasov, byez davadzet minoot.*" Five o'clock, without twenty minutes.

She stood there for a second with a puzzled expression and asked me if I was from Estonia, or maybe Poland. My Russian wasn't authentic enough even for the time of day.

After a brief conversation, Tamara, who spoke some English, offered to show me around Kalinin. I liked the possibility of a tour guide, but I wondered if someone wanted to know what I was doing driving around in the Russian countryside. Why not send a young woman to find out? I decided to not let that bother me. Even if she was an informer, it would be a cheap way to see Kalinin. Intourist would have charged me over one hundred American dollars. But, in retrospect, at least they wouldn't have tried to kill me in my rented car.

Tamara told me she was a member of Komsomol, the communist youth party. She asked a lot of questions, like why I had come to the USSR alone? Was I a Republican or a Democrat? She'd never heard of an independent voter. We walked along the Volga chatting for a couple hours. I think we were both enjoying the exchange.

She invited me to her parents' apartment for dinner. We rode a creaking elevator up to the seventh floor of a Soviet apartment building from the Khrushchev era. A lot of the city had been destroyed in World War II, and most of the buildings had been constructed since then. We stepped out of the elevator. Tamara's mother greeted us at a red vinyl-covered door that opened into a hallway, past a kitchen. A small, friendly woman, she wiped her hands on a towel before welcoming me to her home.

The apartment seemed large by Russian standards. Two bedrooms opened into a well-furnished living room, crowded with an upright grand piano, stuffed chairs, a couch, a Central Asian tapestry wall hanging, and a glass case of Chinese ceramics. Glass doors opened onto a balcony. Tamara made me a tape of underground Russian rock music on her Japanese cassette player.

Her family clearly had advantages beyond average Soviet citizens. Tamara had traveled in Hungary and Italy with a girlfriend and wore Western jeans. I noticed a color brochure for Porsche pinned on the wall of her room.

Tamara was friendly and charming, but aloof. When talking about politics, she always switched over to Russian and spoke very quickly, without much eye contact. I wondered if I was hearing rhetoric. She obviously didn't care if I understood or not, although she had spoken in English when we were walking in downtown Kalinin. She had pointed to the red banners that decorated buildings with party slogans like, "Glory to the People" and "Hard work builds Socialism."

"Reading these words every day doesn't make me want to work harder, or feel like a better person," she said. "People don't pay any attention to these signs. I think they're not necessary."

Tamara seemed disenchanted with her work as a computer programmer, if that's what she really did. She told me she wanted to be a tour guide for English-speaking groups. Before she could switch professions, though, she owed the state four years of work in her field in exchange for her free education.

As I sat on the couch trying out her brother's electric guitar and sipping Cuban rum, the door from the kitchen-hallway slid open. A severe looking, tall, husky man walked in wearing a Soviet Army officer's uniform under a long trench coat. He didn't remove his gold braided hat but walked directly over to me without smiling. My year in military school made me jump up quickly in response to the uniform. Tamara's father reached his hand out and said something. I didn't listen. I was too preoccupied by his intensity.

"Pleased to meet you," I replied, wagging on the end of his grip. He nodded, turned, and left the room. I turned nervously to Tamara.

"What was that all about?"

"That was Papa," Tamara said, grinning at my concern. "He saw a foreigner's car downstairs and wondered who from another country would come to this apartment building. Then he found you in his home. You are the first foreigner to ever be in his home. And he welcomed you."

I thought he'd just given me five minutes to get out of town.

As we drove along the highway that night near the outskirts of Kalinin, a lighted Soviet traffic control tower appeared in the distance. Trouble ahead.

"Tamara, we can't go by that tower!" I pointed down the road. "My passport and driver's license are at the campsite."

"Don't worry." Tamara kept driving. She didn't seem to care.

"No, you don't understand. They'll stop the car. It has foreign plates!"

The tower was getting larger by the second. I could see a policeman sitting in the window. A foreigner without ID, heading out into the countryside at midnight, with a young Komsomol woman. It wasn't going to look good.

"Turn around. We must!"

"Don't worry," she said.

I surrendered and slumped back in the seat. I wished I had never let her drive the car. None of this would be happening to me. She slowed fifty yards before the tower, then turned sharply off the highway onto another road.

"This road leads to your campsite," she said.

"Oh."

I felt a little stupid, but angry that she hadn't told me what was happening. How was I supposed to know? When Tamara stopped at the campground, she looked at her watch and told me she'd missed the last bus by five minutes.

"Can you give me a ride home?" she asked. "Or will it be too difficult to find your way back?"

I didn't believe her. It seemed absurd after driving me all the way here. She probably just wanted to drive the car again.

Kalinin was a city of more than four hundred thousand people. Tamara lived on the far side of the urban center. It took me half an hour to drive back to her folks' apartment. This time, I memorized the route.

We pulled up under a streetlamp, and she started to write her address on a piece of paper so I could mail her a postcard from the States.

An older woman came running out of the darkness with a look of terror on her face. She was crying and holding herself with both arms across her chest. My first thought was rape. Tamara talked with her. The woman was having severe chest pains. She needed a hospital, and my car was the only one in sight. Tamara opened the back door for her, then held her hand and spoke quietly to her. We raced across the city, the woman breathing heavily, quietly sobbing in the back seat. She had vomited on herself. I rolled the window down for fresh air.

Now it was my turn to drive a hundred kilometers an hour through neighborhoods. I disobeyed the law and used headlights. Tamara gave me sharp commands on where to turn. The hospital looked vacant when we pulled up. Only a few lights were on.

"*Spasiba, spasiba bolshoi!*" the woman cried. Thank you, thank you very much!

Tamara opened the car door and walked with the woman along a sidewalk to the emergency room door. The woman was still holding her chest as she disappeared into the hospital. A nurse was near the door.

"That's all we can do," Tamara said. "The doctors will take care of her. Let's go."

I made it back to the campsite at one o'clock in the morning, and the gate was locked. I banged and shook the metal gate until a grumbling attendant finally came out in his nightshirt to open the padlock.

I couldn't get to sleep. I just stared at the walls of the tent cabin, watching insomnia theater replay the roller coaster ride, without headlights, and a desperate woman in the night.

One of Tamara's comments stayed with me. I had asked her if she was happy living in the Soviet Union.

"Am I happy with my life? No, not all the time. Sometimes I am really happy. But other times I'm not happy at all and I don't know why. I just feel sad. Tell me, are people happy all the time in America?"

A cluster of semi-trucks jamming the parking lot of a roadside restaurant seemed a good recommendation for lunch. I made a quick U-turn across the narrow, two-lane highway. Colorful ceramic tiles and varnished trim boards decorated the facade of the country diner.

I took a window table. Several drivers were eating lunch and talking. They probably had a few stories about breakdowns and gas lines. Near Kalinin, I'd seen about forty trucks lined up at the gas pumps.

A waitress walked over and rattled off the day's menu and waited for me to order. She didn't seem in a hurry as she gazed out the window. My orange Zhiguli was the only car in the parking lot. With its black-trimmed interior and gold license plates, it looked like a ladybug in the midst of the big olive-green tractor trailers.

To avoid confusion in ordering, since I hadn't understood much of what she said, I pointed to the next table where a big burly man wearing boots, jeans and a plaid work-shirt sat hunched over a plate of food.

"I want that, please."

"Tea?"

"Da."

"*Spasiba*," the woman said quietly, with an amused smile.

The diner didn't look like a place where foreigners stopped. It was a long way from the Metropol restaurant on Karl Marx Street in Moscow. It seemed closer to a trucker's cafe about a hundred miles down the road from my home, called Janet's Cafe, although I doubted this place served cheeseburgers or had Hank Williams on a jukebox.

A three-course meal arrived, balanced across the waitress's arms and fingers. Cabbage soup, cucumber salad and a beef cutlet with bread and potatoes. In the land of tea drinkers, the waitress didn't have a coffee pot handcuffed to her wrist.

During lunch, I watched a group of drivers in the parking lot. A semi was jacked up, and a man without a shirt worked feverishly wrestling the duals off the rear axle. His back glistened with perspiration, and his hands and arms were smudged with grease. The other drivers assisted him.

I'd seen a lot of roadside repairs along Russian highways, but never a tow truck. If a rig broke down, other drivers stopped to help. I'd also noticed that Soviet motorists were pretty good at breaking a tire off a rim and patching it alongside the road, then remounting it and pumping it full of air. My rented car came with tire irons and a hand pump in the trunk.

I paid my bill and walked out to the car at the same time as the burly driver in the plaid shirt. He asked me where I was from, and then wanted to know who I thought would be the next U.S. president after the November elections. We stood and talked in the parking lot for a few minutes before he climbed up into the cab of his Soviet-built Kamaz tractor trailer rig. A few minutes later, I heard the howl of a starter motor and watched a black cloud of smoke blow from the exhaust stack as the truck lurched back onto the highway.

I pulled back out onto the narrow, two-lane highway and pointed the car north. I'd expected that the main highway connecting Moscow and Leningrad would be at least four lanes, maybe a turnpike. These are the two largest cities in the USSR, similar to New York and Boston. But, once out of the city, the road was just two lanes, sometimes without a white painted divider line.

And there were no white lines indicating the shoulder side of the lane, either. Just a black asphalt blob, with trucks, buses, and cars hurtling forward from the opposite direction, and sometimes a few goats and sheep might be crossing the road, just to keep you alert. At night it was worse.

The main highway between Moscow and Leningrad in 1984

When I pulled into the campground outside Novgorod, the place appeared locked up for the season. All the tent cabins were taken down, and there were no cars or people in sight. I drove up to a small, one-room office and found a caretaker. I handed him my camping voucher and waited expectantly. I thought I might be at the wrong campground.

The guy stood there looking at the government camping voucher and at me and back at the voucher. He knew I was a foreigner. He was trying to figure out what to do with me. I didn't have a sleeping bag. The tent cabins were supposed to have all that gear. But it was all shut down.

"We're closed for the year," he said, as if that would solve his problem.

"Where do I stay then?" I asked.

"*Neznayou, fsyo zacrete.*" I don't know, everything is closed. He emphasized the work closed.

I refused to leave. I just stood there, letting him know that I was now his problem. He hemmed and hawed a bit, scratched his head, then looked over at a large dormitory-type building outside the camp area.

"Over there." He pointed at the dormitory. "There are rooms."

Things were looking up.

We went to the building and parked out front. I was skeptical since there were no cars or people in sight again, but I followed him inside.

The place was not set up for tourism, or for anything for that matter. It looked like it was built in the 1940s and had never been maintained. He led me up wooden stairs to a second floor, down a hallway and showed me a room. It was littered with debris and a stack of mattresses.

"What else is there?" I asked. I noticed about a dozen young Soviet soldiers drinking vodka and bantering farther down the hall. They eyed me, curiously.

"How's this?" my guide asked.

The next room had a steel bed, a mattress and a light bulb hanging on a chain. It looked like the window hadn't been opened in some years and the room hadn't been painted since Stalin was in power. I walked over to the bathroom and saw a toilet broken off at the floor. There was no running water. But that hadn't stopped people from using the broken toilet.

"I think I'll look for something else," I said.

I pointed the Zhiguli back out onto the highway, drove to a downtown Novgorod Intourist hotel and let the manager know that I was now his problem. He proved more creative than the campground caretaker. He gave me a nice room with a view in exchange for my camping voucher.

The color TV buzzed and fluttered for five minutes before it warmed up. I don't know what I expected to find on the Soviet tube at eight o'clock in the evening in the eleven-hundred-year-old city of Novgorod, but certainly not Burt Reynolds. Yet, there he was, speaking fluent Russian. A couple days before, I'd seen the marquee of a Leningrad movie theater on Nevsky Prospekt, advertising *The Verdict* with Paul Newman.

I flipped the station. Rows of combines roared impressively across grain fields in Ukraine. Happy farmers talked about harvesting the crops. I couldn't understand what they said, but I watched for a few minutes before turning it off and heading for the streets. The last sunset colors faded into darkness.

Outside the hotel, a few young men milled around a small plaza. When I crossed the street, one of them broke out of the group and walked quickly toward me, falling in alongside.

"Do you know what time it is?" he asked in Russian. He was tall, with bushy blond hair. His question belied his black-market intentions.

"*Da.*" I pulled my sleeve back, taking the bait and revealing my digital watch. "Eight-thirty." I tried to say the time casually so he would think I was Russian and leave me alone. But he knew I was a foreigner before I opened my mouth. I'd been easily recognized me as I exited the Intourist Hotel in my silver and gray Hi-Tec walking shoes. Novgorod didn't have the cosmopolitan atmosphere of Moscow. It was an old provincial city made dreary by rain clouds and neglect.

Gazirovannaya Voda - Carbonated water vending machines

The marketeer walked with me down the street, frisking me for my nationality and destination, speaking enough English to say that he wanted to buy my shoes, pants, and watch.

He kept asking how much my clothes cost in America. He liked my shoes, which probably seemed like glass slippers on the streets of Novgorod. I felt the guilty stab of having too much and wanted this sidewalk conversation to end. I'd encountered very few speculators in the five weeks I'd been in Russia. Wearing Soviet shirts and sandals helped me blend into crowds. These streetwise businesspeople moved with the wariness of sidewalk drug dealers in America. Soviet law prohibited speculating in foreign goods and currency, but a lot of people did it anyway.

The tall youth continued walking alongside me until I pointedly told him, "*Ooo menye nyet vyeshee prodavat.*" I have no things to sell.

He nodded, peeled off and jogged back toward his friends. I felt relieved, but my conscience was uneasy. The guy obviously didn't have much. His sneakers were falling apart, and his jeans were worn. A lot of young men his age in America already had new cars. He'd left a beat-up, undersized bicycle leaning next to a tree when he came over to me.

I walked downtown and ended up in the city park after dark. A mixed group of old and young people danced around a fountain to a few accordion players squeezing folk tunes out of their instruments. I sat and watched their light-footed polka steps before continuing down a dark, tree-lined path toward the river.

A crowd of teenagers had gathered outside an open-air music arena. High wooden walls surrounded the pavilion, and a rock band echoed from inside. The ticket booth was a large, windowless box the size of four telephone booths, with a mousehole opening at belt level for transactions. Concertgoers placed their coins in the curved opening and a hand reached out and snatched the money. All you could see were the fingertips.

The person inside the booth mimicked my accent in a high voice, then laughed. That didn't do much for my sense of success at blending into the crowd. I'd only said, "One ticket, please."

A platoon of older men wearing red armbands supervised the dark arena entrance. A few low-wattage light bulbs cast a dim glow on their faces. A muscular guy in a tight-fitting shirt used a stiff shoulder to bump me aside. The faint smell of liquor lingered in his wake. I held up my ticket, and one of the red armbands nodded me past.

The lights of Novgorod reflected overhead against low evening clouds. Four or five hundred teenagers crowded the pavilion floor, dancing conservatively to a seven-piece, electrified, folk rock group. The lead singer played acoustic guitar and sang through an echo chamber.

After each song, a few people clapped and hooted, but most remained quiet. I was used to noisy American concert crowds. It felt strange to be around several hundred teenagers and to have the scuffing of shoes be the loudest sound between songs.

The whole arena was dimly lit, so it was hard to see faces. Red armbands stood stiffly in the shadows watching, while black leather and denim danced to Russian rock.

When the band took a break, several films played across a large screen mounted on a wall. An anti-smoking cartoon showed the devil making everybody smoke, corrupting people's health, and instigating industrial pollution that ruined the environment. Just about every teenager in the place lit up a cigarette while the cartoon played, laughing and blowing smoke at the devil's antics.

In the other film, a teenager from a broken home got punched out by a gang of hooligans. The punky gang leader wore a tight-fitting U.S. Marines T-shirt. The crowd loved it.

When the band started playing again, I moved over to a dark wall at the far side of the arena and stood on a bench for a better view of the stage and crowd. I'd been up there about ten seconds when a stern, older woman with a red armband showed up out of the shadows and poked me in the arm.

"*Nyet!*"

She disappeared as soon as both my feet touched the floor. I walked out to the edge of the dance floor and leaned against a pole, half expecting a poke in the ribs.

Instead, one of the dancers in front of me dropkicked some guy in the side of the face with his boot. The fight spread quickly. In a flash, ten people were kicking and punching in front of me. I stepped back. One group broke off to the side of me. Three guys fighting two. Head punches and Kung Fu feet.

One person went down. Then a stocky, red armband came flying out of the shadows, blitzing like a linebacker through the melee, swinging his elbows and straight-arming a couple guys unlucky enough to be in his path. A few of the teenagers got knocked to the ground. The fight stopped. Someone on the floor got a last-minute kick in the ribs. The dancing froze, then resumed. The band never stopped.

I stood back against the wall. A tall, shadowy figure in a black leather jacket and bushy hair walked up to me in the darkness, nodded his head, doubled up both fists, and made a whirling motion with his hands. I felt a rush of adrenaline. He either wanted to fight or was motioning about the fight that had just occurred. I didn't know, and it was too dark to see his eyes clearly. I watched his hands. He yelled something at me. The music was too loud, and I couldn't hear. He stepped toward me. I thought he was going to take a swing, but he bent his head close to my ear.

"*Pomneesh menye? Strachali na gostaneetsoo.*" He shouted over a blaring guitar solo. Remember me? We met at the hotel.

The black-marketeer. I didn't recognize him in the dark. The lights were behind him, revealing very little of his face.

"*Tantsovat?*" He spun his fists again in the whirling motion, asking me if I wanted to dance with him.

"*Da, tantsovat,*" I yelled back reluctantly. We stepped out to the dance floor. He grinned in an odd way. I couldn't tell if he was assessing me, or if it was the bad lighting. Then I noticed four or five others dancing around us. His friends. They'd been in the fight. The marketeer danced loosely. He leaned over and told one of his friends something. They passed it around and grinned as they watched me.

"You are here alone?" he asked, looking down at my shoes.

"*Da.*" I didn't feel like dancing anymore.

"You leave to Leningrad tomorrow?" he asked.

I nodded, watching what his friends were up to. The back of my shoulders felt knotted. My mind raced ahead. It was a long walk back to the hotel, down dark streets.

"Come on, let's go." The tall guy motioned toward the exit. I balked.

"Where to?"

"To my girlfriend, there." He pointed across the arena to the doors. He sensed my discomfort. "I want you to meet my girlfriend, please."

We walked around the crowd. I watched his friends. They nodded goodbye, still dancing in a cluster. In a few seconds I lost sight of them in the shadows. All the dark figures blended in together. We stopped near the stage.

"Please, wait, I have to talk to someone. Don't go away." He disappeared into the crowd again.

I thought about making a quick break for the door but decided to stick around and see what would happen. The marketeer returned with his girlfriend. She extended her hand toward me with a shy, pleasant smile and said hello. They both took me by the elbow and insisted I dance with them to a fast rock song. I relaxed a little and began to almost trust him.

The next song was slow. I walked over to the edge of the stage and watched the guitar player while the couple danced together. But my mind was distracted by a dialogue between my departments of internal security and external affairs.

When the slow dance ended, I told them I was leaving. I lied and said it was only because I had to get up early for the drive to Leningrad. The night had been too weird. I was starting to trust the situation but still felt jittery, like it could all go wrong in a second. They wished me a good trip. We shook hands, and I left.

Outside the arena, I slipped off onto a dark path, taking a different direction back to the hotel. I moved quickly, glancing back over my shoulder. It was difficult to see anything in the soot-black tree shadows.

Catherine's Palace in Tsarskoe Selo, near Leningrad

The accordion music still hummed near the fountain. The folk dancers were still singing traditional songs. Their simplicity appealed to me. I walked along a main sidewalk. It was about one o'clock in the morning. The last buses of the night roared along the boulevard. The clouds had thinned. I cut across a parking lot and a big grassy field, walking by moonlight along a levy near my hotel.

I wondered if Burt Reynolds had ever heard himself speak fluent Russian.

My birthday was off to a bad start. The weather in Leningrad had cooled under a heavy drizzle, and the campground's communal hot water system had failed. After taking a cold shower on a concrete floor, I walked shivering back to the tent cabin. At least the tent cabins were still functioning in Leningrad, unlike in Novgorod.

Then I noticed yet another flat tire. I'd just gotten the last flat repaired. My orange Zhiguli didn't like me anymore. The previous day, a loud snap in the transmission finished off the reverse gear, leaving me with four speeds forward and no options to back up. A traffic cop had fined me five rubles for not having my seatbelt fastened at an intersection in Leningrad. I needed good news.

After changing the flat tire in the rain, I decided to drive to the city ferry station and take the *Raketa* hydro-foil ferry to Petrodvorets—Peter the Great's Palace.

I waited at the pier on the Neva River for an hour and a half, but the boat didn't come. A man with a fishing pole and no fish told me the ferries had stopped running because of winds and heavy rain. I decided to try the car.

My downward spiral had started a few days before in the city of Yaroslavl, about one hundred and sixty miles north of Moscow. I had started feeling sick and had had a violent coughing spell in the periodicals section of a library. Everyone in the room watched me try to escape out the door past an irate librarian who barred my passage, verbally berating me. She had made an example of me for not checking my shoulder bag at the front desk when I'd entered the place.

I guess she thought I might be stealing magazines. My red face and hacking foreign accent won an instant apology, but I felt sick and degraded when I stepped back outside into the rain.

Half an hour later, I found an *aptyeka*, a Russian drug store. I hoped to find something on the shelf for my cough, but the shelves were metal racks filled with dried herbs. I spotted some prescription-type meds on a shelf as well, behind the counter.

Being sick on the far side of the planet worried me. The *aptyeka* appeared to function more on descriptions than prescriptions. People in line would describe things, then the attendant would select various remedies.

"I have a cough," I told the young woman behind the counter, "and my head is hot and crazy."

She asked questions that I couldn't understand, grinning and raising her eyebrows at a co-worker, then handed me some little pink pills, some white ones, and a bottle of eucalyptus cough medicine, for thirty-five kopecks.

"Two of these every four hours," she said, holding one of the pills up in front of my nose. "And one of these three times a day. Do you understand?"

"Yes." I should have written it down. By the time I got back to my modest hotel room, I forgot which pill was which, so I took four, every four hours and ended up feeling dizzy. But the cough and fever went away quickly.

I drove west through the streets of Leningrad, windshield wipers slapping back and forth, trying to follow a folded, six-inch, photocopied map that I'd found at a kiosk on the street, representing twenty square miles of old-world metropolitan sprawl. Like a spiderweb, the streets made abstract connections, among oddly shaped blocks of buildings intersected by scores of canals. American cities seemed like simple checkerboards compared to the jigsaw puzzle of Russian streets.

Some street signs in downtown Leningrad were fastened to the corners of buildings set back about thirty feet from the curb and often hidden behind large trees. Frequently, I would have to park the car and run over under the trees to see what a street sign said. I continued along main boulevards until I was off the map and into the intuitive zone. A flashing red light on the gas gauge signaled problems yet to come. I hadn't seen a gas station for a couple of days.

Half an hour later I spotted several gas pumps secluded behind a row of small trees. Five or six cars sat in line at the low-octane pumps. When I rented the car, I'd received high-octane gas coupons. I had the feeling that those weren't available to the average local motorist. Most Soviet drivers bought the cheap stuff. I drove past the string of cars to the self-serve high-octane pump, where there was no line.

"Forty liters." I shoved my gas coupons through the small, glass opening to the cashier. She examined them, then switched on the pump.

With a full tank of gas, I approached a road sign that read "Tallinn and the Republic of Estonia." An arrow pointed up into the sky. Another arrow with three roads to choose from pointed toward Petrodvorets.

For the next hour, I drove in circles, stopping periodically to quiz people on the street: "Where is Petrodvorets?" One woman didn't know what I was talking about, and another sent me down the road to Estonia. A couple of rain-soaked teenaged hitchhikers pointed me back toward Leningrad. An over-animated gentleman intricately described his neighborhood, pointed his fingers, made sweeping hand gestures, and bulged out his eyes hoping to enlighten me.

I listened cautiously to a fat man who gave me directions while brushing the coat of a monstrous thing that was chained and baring its fangs at me. Then I met a policeman who sensed my uncertain grasp of the Russian language and spoke to me as if I were a moron, pointing out that a small section of the road to Petrodvorets was closed for repair and that an unmarked detour was in effect.

Sheets of heavy rain started to fall again. I hoped I wouldn't get another flat tire since I no longer had a spare. I'd gotten more flat tires in two weeks on Russian roads than I had in the last ten years at home. Peering out the windows, looking for even a hint of the palace, I almost ran over an unmarked, open manhole in the middle of the street.

After a while, I began to think that every driver knew where to go but me. My American highway sense had been groomed by lighted signs, quivers of roadside arrows, and centerline reflectors. I needed instinct to survive on Russian streets.

Finally, I saw some intriguing ten-foot-high yellow walls, but no sign. I parked my car and asked a man standing in front of a small market, "Where's Petrodvorets?" He pointed over my shoulder toward the yellow walls. I felt like a dope standing in front of Mt. Rushmore asking where Lincoln's head was.

I followed a side street, walked through a gate, turned a few corners, and saw a small Cyrillic sign: "Entrance. 30 kopecks."

My mood suddenly brightened as I shelled out the kopecks to buy a ticket and an ice cream bar. I should have used my pocket dictionary to translate the fine print posted at the cashier's window. Tickets varied in price, so I bought the cheapest one and entered the grounds feeling victorious.

The sun broke through the afternoon clouds as I strolled through the palace forests, looking at scores of fountains and golden statues, canals, and gardens.

One fountain resembled a giant colorful mushroom. Forty people could stand under its cap. Hundreds of waterjets ringed the sculpture, forming a circular curtain of water. No one knew when the jets would erupt. Sometimes they went on and off in seconds, and sometimes minutes. People, mostly children, would dart back and forth from the cover of the mushroom, daring a good soaking.

My first leap ended in a dry landing. From under the cap, the jets of water looked like glass columns, an inch or two apart. Several children jumped back and forth, completely soaked, shrieking with laughter every time they got doused. I thought about it too long on the way out and walked around the rest of the day with a wet pant leg.

The winds had subsided, and the hydro-foil ferries began to arrive from downtown Leningrad. Most people came to Petrodvorets by water, landing at the convenient piers where the palace grounds met the Gulf of Finland. I had arrived at the back door.

Peter had an impressive palace. The Nazis enjoyed it so much in the forties that they took most of the statues, art, and other antiques back to Germany when they went home. They also trashed the mansion. The Russians had to conquer Berlin to get their treasures back. The government spent millions of rubles to put Peter's house back in order.

I decided to have lunch in an outdoor restaurant on the grounds before touring the palace itself. It was a palace *stolovaya*, a large cafeteria with outdoor seating near the trees and canal. A good lunch cost less than a ruble.

Four Romani women sat at the other end of the table, taking a lunch break from peddling their silver and leather work to palace visitors. I think their peddling was against the law. One of them had accosted me earlier on a remote path on the palace grounds park and practically grabbed me by the shirt collar to get me to buy something. She didn't seem to remember me.

When I finally decided to see the palace, I discovered that my cheap ticket didn't cover the cost of an inside tour. The ticket booth was closed by then. I tried to sneak in, but a sixty-year-old, iron-willed woman guard wouldn't let me into the inner corridors without a ticket. I'd even managed to get a pair of the required slippers for my shoes to protect the inlaid wood floors. The guard barred my passage with folded arms and a head that swiveled back and forth. I acted disoriented, spoke only in English, and handed her an old ticket stub from the Moscow circus.

"*Nyet.*" She was a veteran.

One of the directors, a bushy-haired younger man with horn-rimmed glasses, asked what country I was from. He smiled, shrugged his shoulders, and turned me away, too, but without conviction.

As I walked away feeling rejected, he reappeared through a side door out of sight of the older woman. He motioned quickly to me. I followed him through a series of dark passages that led upstairs through the walls of the palace. He nodded to me and opened another door, turning me loose on the second floor of the palace for a self-guided tour. I'd finally reached Petrodvorets.

The old Petropavlovsk Fortress was a quiet spot to spend an afternoon. Stone walls rose to seal out the city's noise, and the dark waters of the Neva River lapped against the buttress of quarried footings that formed a wide promenade along the fort's southern exposure. A few people leaned against the thick rock walls, absorbing the sun's warmth.

I had just emerged from the Cathedral of the Tsars, after spending an hour with the dead rulers of old Russia. About thirty tsars lay scattered around the floor of the golden-spired cathedral, boxed up in sealed marble vaults surrounded by little fences. Gold Cyrillic nameplates identified each miniature tomb.

A bicyclist at the edge of the promenade caught my attention. He was sitting on the stonework, bent over his newspaper. I walked by him three times, hoping to catch his eye, but he never looked up. He wore black cycling pants, a wool jersey, leather cycling shoes, and a small cap with a stunted bill. I knew we would have something in common. Some people strolled along the river's edge, but there were no other cyclists with racing bikes.

"Excuse me. What kind of bike is that?"

The man looked up. I felt nervous. My Russian sounded odd. He stood up quickly. He was a surprisingly large man, about six feet and four inches, with energetic movements and an athletic build. He looked more like a pro football player than an avid cyclist. He didn't quite understand my question. I asked again.

"*Eta Sovietsky velociped?*" A Soviet bicycle?

"*Da. Sovietsky,*" he answered, glancing at his green ten-speed as if it were only a distraction. "You are foreigner. From what country are you?"

I gave him my usual reply, watching his expression. The man's jaw looked as solid as the stone blocks under our feet.

"*Oohh, Americanetz!* Hello, hello! Please sit down here with me." He quickly folded his newspaper into a little mat and placed it on the smooth, cold stone. I wasn't sure what the paper was intended for and started to sit next to it. He took me by the arm, insisting that I sit on the newspaper. "Where in America?"

"California, near San Francisco."

"Have you lost your group?"

"No, I'm traveling alone."

"Alone! In Russia. Ha!" He slapped his knee. "What a surprise. And you are having a good travel? I am glad to meet you. My name is Alexander. Alexander Nikolaiovich." He shook my hand vigorously. "I'm very glad you are here."

I began to relax. It had been awkward for me to approach the Russian cyclist, who was so engrossed in his reading.

Alexander spoke in sudden bursts of Russian, often too difficult for me to understand. He pointed across the river toward Leningrad's eighteenth-century skyline, telling me that he worked for the city as an electrical technician, mostly on the subway system. He had also worked at the Hermitage, the tsars' ornate Winter Palace, which stretched along the Neva for the length of two football fields. The blue, white, and gold architectural monument now housed one of the world's largest art collections.

He had studied English for six years when he was a young boy in grade school, but he couldn't remember those lessons now. He spoke only in Russian.

"Foreigners in groups from all countries come to the Hermitage," Alexander said. "Once, I tried to talk to an older Englishwoman in my very bad English for practice."

Alexander stuck his nose up in the air and looked down on me with a snobbish, comical expression, twitching his shoulders back and forth imitating the woman. His size made such petite gestures all the funnier. "She looked annoyed that I tried to talk to her. She walked away."

He brought us quickly back to the present. "Do you want to read newspaper?"

"It is too difficult for me," I replied.

"For practice. I will help you! I have another paper."

Alexander stood up and grabbed a cylinder wrapped in newspaper from one of the water bottle holders bolted to his bike frame. He unrolled it. Vodka. Alexander wagged his finger.

"*Nyet, nyet*. This is not for us. I don't drink or smoke. Bad for health." He pounded on his chest with a fist, then scooted around to face me, sticking out his chin and posing like a statue. "How old do you think I am?"

I studied his face for a moment. He was so physically fit it was almost scary. But the way the question was baited, I decided to guess low.

"Thirty-eight."

"Ha, ha!" Alexander Nikolaiovich had a good laugh. "*Nyet*. Forty-seven. It's true! I ride my bike. I don't drink. I don't smoke. This vodka is for my daughter. Today, she is twenty-one years old. Her friends will come to celebrate her birthday."

It was hard to believe Alexander could have a twenty-one-year-old daughter and a teenaged son.

We sat along the Neva talking for a couple of hours. He read words aloud from the newspaper and tried to explain what the stories were about. Then he prodded me to read the long, grammatically complicated text and he would correct my pronunciation. After a while, we set the newspaper aside and talked about our lives.

He spoke urgently about our two countries and how we must live as friends, without war.

"*Mir ee druzhba!*" Peace and friendship!

It was happening again. Everywhere, Soviet people insisted that I understand this. Alexander seemed even more emphatic than some of the others. "*Mir ee druzhba*" was starting to sound like a Russian version of "have a good day," except here, people seemed driven by some terrible demon in their past. Most Americans I knew who worked for peace were driven by visions of fire in the future. Soviet cities had already burned in war. Many people had been scarred by the flames.

A Russian policeman in a long gray coat strolled by on his beat.

"In America, police carry guns, yes? And people, too? *Ploxa*." Bad, he said. "Here, police don't need guns. It's not as dangerous to live!" Alexander continued. "But in America, I think you have many products. *Xarasho!* That is very

good." He gave me the thumbs up sign, nodding agreeably. "That is better than here. But I like Leningrad. It is my city! Good air to breathe. Like the country!"

An older woman in a two-piece swimsuit who had been standing in the sun against the fortress wall walked over to us.

"I listen to your conversation." She spoke in Russian. "But I cannot tell what nationality you are. Are you German?"

"No, he is American," Alexander Nikolaiovich said.

"Ohh!" Her face became serious. "We don't want war. Your president speaks with jokes about war." Before I could respond, she held up her right arm. It was covered with scars. She clasped her wrinkled hands together and then released them like an explosion, a sharp sound in her breath. Bombs. She pantomimed small pieces of metal entering her body. Shrapnel. The woman put her right foot forward. It was maimed, twisted to the right.

"From war," she hissed. Her expression was haunted as she spoke of the war. "I was on the front in Leningrad. Three years! I was lucky. I lived. Many didn't. I helped soldiers fight. Many died."

Alexander listened quietly as the woman narrated her story. Her memories of war plagued her.

"Yes, I remember those days, too," Alexander spoke up, surprising me. He seemed too young. "I was five years old when the war started. Eight years old when it ended. Sometimes, all we had to eat was grass, pulled from the dirt. I don't ever want to live that again. And I don't want my children to, either."

The woman returned to the fortress wall and sorted through her purse. She came back with something in her hands.

"Here," she offered, "presents for you. Please take these."

She handed me two colorful wallet-sized calendars from Leningrad. I thanked her. Her story had planted itself in my mind. I felt fortunate to be there.

I coughed slightly. Alexander jumped up quickly as she retreated back to the wall.

"Don't sit on the ground." He was concerned. "You coughed. You need warmth. Be strong in your health." Alexander hoisted me up by the arm and guided me over to the sun-warmed wall. I felt like I was about six years old and had just coughed in front of my mother. A cool breeze blew along the Neva from the Gulf of Finland. I hoped I wouldn't cough again. Alexander would probably throw me over his shoulder and carry me to the hospital.

"I am interested to know," Alexander said, "What do the older people in America say about Soviet Union?"

"Some are curious about life here. And others are afraid or think it's bad. They don't like the political system of the USSR."

"Here, I think there are people like that, too." Alexander laughed a little, but it was an uneasy laugh.

The woman interrupted her sunbathing again and walked over to us. "Take him to *Marsovo Polye*. He should see that." She held both of my hands between hers.

"Okay." Alexander nodded.

I drove my car across Kirovsky Bridge, following Alexander as he pedaled his bicycle quickly in the flow of traffic. He stopped near a park, and we crossed the street to an expansive war memorial garden the size of a large city block. A wide walkway led to the center of the memorial garden. Alexander grew silent as we approached the stone monument.

A wedding group arrived and walked quietly to the site to lay flowers and stand in silence before a small eternal flame. Alexander whispered to me, "A tradition. Everyone who marries brings flowers. To never forget those who had to die." In numerous cities, I'd seen wedding parties lay flowers at war memorials.

Almost as an afterthought, Alexander leaned back toward me. "More than nine hundred thousand people died in Leningrad during the war."

I stood for a second, translating the Russian numbers in my head. Then they hit me. Hard. Alexander's words welled up out of the earth and through the bottoms of my feet. Just as if every woman, man, and child in San Francisco were gone—and then some. Alexander was a little boy eating grass for food while the bombs fell. One thousand people dying every day. Every single day for three years. The old woman, a bloodied teenager in the trenches. They'd told me their stories. I just stood there and let the chills pass through me, like I had in the fields of Gettysburg. Over six hundred thousand Americans killed in the Civil War. Twenty million Soviet deaths in World War II. I'd read the statistics in books and found them impossible to comprehend. But now they were touching me.

Alexander nudged my elbow and motioned to go. We didn't talk again until we'd crossed the street and entered a park shadowed by trees in fall color. A little girl skipped by wearing a crown of meticulously hand-tied autumn leaves balanced on her head. Her lighthearted movement welcomed me back from the ruminations of war.

I looked over at Alexander. He was right at my elbow, walking his bicycle with his other hand. We strolled the length of the park, teaching each other the English and Russian words for everything we encountered, from drinking fountains and benches to artists' easels and snack bars. We followed a canal waterway back to my car.

"Oh, oh," Alexander cautioned. "*Militzia,*" he laughed quietly, pointing across the street. My car was parked illegally. A policeman with tall black boots stood waiting alongside.

"Problem?"

"*Nyet,*" Alexander hushed. "Just wait. He'll get frustrated and leave." He thought it was funny.

We sat down on a park bench and watched the policeman. The officer became agitated, looking at his watch and all around the lawns for the driver of the car. He put one of his black boots on the bumper, then both feet on the sidewalk. He twitched a black and white traffic wand around in his hand. He wanted to write a ticket.

I told Alexander that in America a truck would come and take the car. It would cost a lot of dollars to get it back.

"No worry," Alexander assured me, "here that doesn't happen." The policeman slowly paced up and down the sidewalk, then finally tired of the wait and continued along his beat. Alexander checked his watch. "I must go. My daughter is expecting her friends in fifteen minutes. I must not be late."

We walked together out onto the street. The policeman was nowhere in sight. Alexander reached out and shook my hand, holding my elbow firmly at the same time. He maintained eye contact with me as he said farewell.

"When you go home, tell your friends that here we want to live in peace. For all time." The flame of *Marsovo Polye* flickered in the distance.

I walked briskly along Leningrad's busy streets, looking for the music theater. Before leaving Moscow, Alex had given me the ticket to an Aquarium concert, a band at the top of the USSR underground music scene. He said, "Don't lose it. You won't be able to buy another." There would be no posters or advertisements. Just word of mouth and tickets distributed by hand, person to person, through an underground layer of Soviet rock music fans.

Aquarium had had a history of playing secret venues since 1972, drawing crowds, pushing the envelope on lyrical content and social sentiment. The Soviet government did not approve of their music, but they were tolerated, unofficially. Their style combined roots of Russian folk music, Western pop, reggae, and other international influences. Their bootlegged cassette tapes were legendary in the USSR and would spread across the entire country in just a few weeks when made available.

As I hurried along the streets, my anticipation was building, similar to attending big U.S. concerts. I expected to encounter crowds, scalpers, lines at the entrance and a band waiting backstage in a secure area for the concert to begin. I knew the drill.

At first, I'd thought about attempting to contact Aquarium about my joint music idea after Alex gave me the ticket. But the band just seemed too big and too popular to approach. It would be like reaching out to the Beatles or Paul Simon. I decided it was best to just go to the concert.

When I arrived at the theater, the doors were open and people were casually walking around. The inner doors to the stage area were locked, but the entrance hall doors were all open. There were no scalpers to be seen. No posters. No frenzied crowd or lines. People were just waiting, talking with each other. It was completely laid back.

After about thirty minutes, the Aquarium band walked in through the front door of the theater building and plopped down on some couches. I recognized the band's leader, Boris Grebenshchikov from photos. Nobody paid much attention to them. Just a few friends walked over and chatted.

I was dumbfounded. No limousines. They probably came on the metro. No fans going berserk to get a glimpse of one of the biggest names in Soviet rock music, in a nation of almost three hundred million people. There was no frenzy at all. Just a group of musicians sitting on a couch chatting casually among themselves and with a few friends, waiting for the theater to officially open.

After an hour, things suddenly changed.

The band disappeared toward the stage area. The crowd began to swell and undulate toward the entrance doors to the inner theater. I was right in the middle of a few hundred people. It was the wrong place to be. The doors were still locked.

The crowd suddenly surged forward, generating a wave that almost knocked me off my feet. People began grabbing each other to stay upright. It was total chaos. The energy hit the wall, then washed back through the crowd, catching me in its undertow.

Then the doors swung open. The wave surged forward again, through the open passageway. People began elbowing their way into the hall and up to the stage area. Now it was beginning feel like the American rock concerts I was used to. But once inside, a more congenial crowd mood returned. Aquarium stepped on stage, led by Grebenshchikov, who said a few words before the band launched into their first song. It would be an unforgettable concert.

Two older *babushkas*, with scarves over their heads, sat on a wooden bench beneath a shade tree, about twenty paces back from the roadside. One woman flicked a long, crooked switch at a small flock of white geese nibbling in the grass at her feet. The corrugated metal roof and split-log gable of a house peeked over a weathered plank fence behind them. Tin buckets filled with apples and potatoes, placed near the base of the tree, were intended for motorists driving across the countryside toward Kalinin, Moscow, and Leningrad.

When I got out of the car, the woman with the switch in her hand stood up slowly and shuffled across the grass to meet me. She wore a scarf over her head, a faded sweater, and rubber boots. Her neighbor nodded my way and walked down a dirt path toward a green and white house next door. All of the homes in the neighborhood had fences and large trees around them.

"*Zdrastvweetye.*" The small, stooped *babushka* greeted me with the slow cadence of her country dialect. She had a face like a withered apple.

"Hello," I replied. "Did you grow these in your garden?"

"*Da, vweerashevayou etix.*" She nodded with a proud smile. The deep lines in her face drew back into new patterns. She reached carefully into the mound of apples, brushing their shapes with her fingertips. She selected one and placed it in my hand. The firm, reddish-green apple smelled like a spring blossom. I was sure no pesticide had touched its skin.

"Very good apples. How much do they cost?"

"One ruble and fifty kopecks for all the apples." She held up her fingers to help illustrate their worth. They were the best apples I'd seen in Russia.

"*Da,* I'll buy all the apples."

"*Xotitye kartoshky tozhe?*" Do you want the potatoes, too?

"No, thank you." Twenty-five pounds of potatoes was not ideal for a light traveler.

The old woman looked at me inquisitively. She gestured for a bag. Obviously, I didn't get the bucket. I had to come up with a container.

My soft luggage shoulder bag looked like it would hold a lot of produce, so I dumped all my clothes into the trunk of the car. A packet of California poppy seeds tumbled out. A timely gift.

The old woman loaded apples into my travel bag one at a time. She held one firmly in front of me. I nodded appreciatively and helped her stuff the bag until it wouldn't shut.

We stood and talked for about ten minutes. Each time she made eye contact with me, my shoulders tingled with the delight of standing in the Russian countryside buying produce from a dear *babushka* with transparent blue eyes.

"Here, I want you to have these." I handed her the seed packet. She studied the colorful graphics, unable to read the strange English description of contents. Her finger pointed to the golden flowers on the packet. "These?"

"*Da, da, da.*" I nodded my head. "In the spring, plant these in your garden soil. Then, during summer, beautiful flowers will grow—like they do in California."

"*Spasiba bolshoi.*" She looked appreciative. "Please wait."

The tiny woman picked up her switch and shuffled over to the geese that pecked in the grass. She chirped and hissed at the white birds and gently prodded them along the earthen path toward the front gate of her fenced yard. She gestured for me to follow. I walked slowly at the end of the procession. She herded the six geese through another gate made of small tree limbs nailed together.

"*Pazhalsta, idtee soodah.*" Please come along. She pointed her long, crooked switch along the side of the house toward the back yard. The dirt path was worn hard and smooth by many years of walking back and forth from the house to the garden. Ornately carved wooden window frames adorned her home. A glass vase filled with red and pink flowers stood against white lace curtains on one of the windowsills. Over time, it appeared the house had settled unevenly into the ground, so that it looked like something out of a folk tale.

Past the house, past a large, sheltered stack of split firewood, and beyond a small outhouse, we came to the garden and apple orchard. One section was entirely flowers. She waded into the waist-high patch of color.

"I want to give you some of my flowers. Perhaps you have a friend in Moscow?"

She cut a few daisies and handed them to me, then went slowly along the rows picking others and bunching them in one hand. Puffy clouds raced overhead, alternately splashing the garden in sunlight and shadow. A well stood nearby, with a little roof over it, and a hand-cranked water bucket hung on a rope. The flower scents mixed with the sweet smell of grass from a nearby field where cows grazed. It was so quiet in the farmlands.

"Do you have a family?" I asked.

"*Da.* Two sons." She paused and looked across the flower patch. "They work in Moscow. My husband died in the war, many years ago. How do these look?" She changed the subject, holding up a mixed bouquet of white, purple, and red flowers. "The weather becomes colder now. See, already frost makes them brown." I noticed a faint tinge of discoloration on a few flowers that she hadn't picked, but the ones for me looked perfect. I admired them, honored by the gift.

The old woman walked over to the edge of the garden where I stood and placed her hand on my arm. I expected her to say something about weather or gardens.

"Your president is very rich man, I think. Does he not understand people with little money? To bomb our land. Why is this a joke?" She looked at me intently, unblinking. Her bony hand rested on my arm.

I struggled to respond. She'd seen the news that President Reagan had made an offhand joke that week about the USSR, saying, "The bombing begins in five minutes."

That clip was leaked to the press and had spread globally.

Even in the remote countryside, an old woman with six white geese feared for the world's future. She had lived through war. What could I say to her? She knew life better than I did. The German army had rolled through these fields and her village in the forties, on their way to Moscow and Kalinin. Tank tracks cut deeply into people's memories.

"No war," she repeated, "*Ne voinah.*"

I asked if I could take her photograph, but she declined. She walked with me to my car and wished me a safe journey to Moscow. For the rest of the day, in every village I drove through, I saw her. She was the same person I saw bundled up, standing on street corners and in underground walkways, selling her flowers for a few kopecks to passers-by in the cities.

The highway to Moscow became a backdrop. I could see the only concern in the old woman's eyes when she spoke of war, the kindness in her face as she handed me the bouquet of flowers from her garden. I remembered her light touch on my arm, the gentle flicking of her switch at the six white geese.

Along the Dneiper

I'd read about Igor Tatsl in *Soviet Life* magazine a year before my trip, and now I was riding the city metro on my way to meet him in Kiev, Ukraine. The magazine had helped arrange the meeting. His address and phone number were waiting for me at the front desk of my hotel when I arrived from Odessa. He lived in an outlying district. This was one of those out of the blue, wild ideas.

Igor Tatsl had been tracking the controversial *Snezhnaya Chelovek* for thirty years in Central Asia's Pamir Mountains, in Tajikistan. This Snow Man creature is the equivalent of the North American Sasquatch, or Big Foot, a phenomenon in the Pacific Northwest dating back to the 1800s. I was intrigued by how the pursuit of a similar creature came to be in other parts of the world.

When I rang Tatsl's doorbell at his flat in Kiev that afternoon, I didn't know what to expect, but he had seemed serious in the magazine article. He was a full university professor and a dedicated alpinist who had been leading expeditions into the Pamirs annually for the last three decades, seeking contact with the Snow Man.

Igor energetically welcomed me into his apartment with a smile and a firm handshake. He was probably in his late fifties, stocky, with a full head of thick, reddish hair brushed straight back and a sharply trimmed beard. His eyes sparkled when he looked around the room, but tracked unevenly, with one locked firmly on me and the other looking slightly past me. He led me into his living room. Three other, younger men were sitting around a table, with photographs, footprint molds, and hair samples and accompanied by tea and snacks. They were part of his alpine team. We jumped right into conversations, mostly in Russian, some in broken English.

In Igor Tatsl's (right) Kiev apartment, looking at plaster casts of the snow man's footprints

He claimed to have had an initial contact with a Snow Man when he hiked in the Pamirs after graduating from university decades ago. The brush with the seemingly exotic creature had changed his life. Igor had returned to the Pamirs close to thirty times since then, often spending a month or more, hiking in the remote, high-altitude region, trying to make contact.

Igor said he or somebody from his party had made physical contact with *Snezhnaya Chelovek* five or six times over the years. He described one time that someone had almost fallen apart emotionally from the experience. The long-haired creature always came at night, would sometimes make high-pitched sounds, maybe brush its hand on your skin in the darkness, then disappear, sometimes leaving tracks. Igor and his mountaineering team leader showed me the plaster casts of footprints they'd preserved and the strings of long, dark hair.

We had an enjoyable evening, exploring a shared interest in an elusive creature that seemed to inhabit different remote parts of the world. Igor and his friends shared a sense of humor and an earnest, clear purpose in their multi-decade pursuit.

Big Foot and Sasquatch had been a phenomenon in our region for ages, and in the late fifties, when I was a kid, the local newspaper published a front-page photo of an eighteen-inch footprint. I'd never been a total believer in the whole phenomenon, but at the same time, there seemed to be just enough evidence that I could never absolutely refute it.

Sitting in Igor Tatsl's living room that evening in Kiev with his very focused and fit alpine team leaders, telling me these stories, showing me the artifacts, left me firmly on the fence.

"Why don't you come to the Pamir Mountains with us one summer. Look for the Snow Man with us?" Igor asked.

"I'd love to do that!" I jumped at the offer, if for no other reason just to hike the Pamir Mountains. The Pamirs are in proximity to some of the tallest and most remote mountains in the world, and access had been sequestered behind the Soviet border for decades. I also knew the likelihood of such a trek with Igor and company was a long shot.

"No American has ever been on one of our treks," his lead alpinist said, though some Eastern Europeans had.

When I left Igor Tatsl's apartment late that night, one of his team members walked me back to the metro station. As we crossed a plaza, a woman came running up to us out of the darkness and grabbed my arm, insisting almost hysterically that she knew me. Igor's friend assured her that she did not and removed her hands from my arm, then escorted me to the metro door. It was an unsettling ending to a strange, fascinating evening.

Downtown Kiev, 1984

I walked through the narrow underground passage that wound for nearly a quarter of a mile beneath the Kiev Pechersk Lavra, a historic monastery and museum in the center of Kiev, known as the Monastery of the Caves because its founder had chosen a nearby cave to start his order. Inside the caves, which were linked by the Lavra underground tunnel walkway, were laid to rest ornately dressed, preserved bodies of spiritual seekers. In some caves, two or three bodies might be laid on their backs, side by side, in garments, gowns, and ornate headdresses. I was dawdling behind a tour group, curiously observing all the cave people who lay with varnished complexions, faces up toward the low ceilings of their carved-out sanctuaries. Some of them had been there for a couple of hundred years, preserved from the elements like mummies.

During their lifetimes, they had been artists, chroniclers, and monks, some of whom had lived under the surface of the earth for twenty years at a time, trying to achieve a spiritual state. I had just unofficially attached myself to a tour since individuals were not allowed to walk through the Lavra alone. I mostly wasn't listening to the guide, a trait I'd developed in school, but picked up that the strange corpses with dark brown, leathery skin had names like Nikon, Nestor, and Alimpy.

I wanted to take a photograph, but the guide said, "*Nelzya.*" It's not permitted. She added that nobody could photograph the preserved saints.

I dropped farther back in the narrow, winding passageway until everyone else was out of sight, then discreetly raised my camera. The shutter speed was set for a long exposure, without a flash.

Five saints lay shoulder to shoulder, framed perfectly in my wide-angle lens. I just needed to focus and hold my breath.

A sharp, burning pain zapped me in the back of the head. I almost dropped the camera. A wasp had stung me. Then it chased me through the passage, vanishing only as I rejoined the group. My head throbbed while the tour guide talked. The five saints remained unphotographed. It could not be done.

I would never forget how I met Anatoly and Valentina in downtown Kiev that day in 1984. I'd just arrived in Kiev after a week at the Black Sea resort of Sochi, in southern Russia, and a few days in Odessa, in southern Ukraine. I was wandering around in central Kiev, a city of more than two million people. I'd been walking miles since sunrise, traversing the historic metropolitan center, strolling along the Dneiper River, crossing bridges, touring the Lavra's underground tunnel of buried saints, standing at the edge of the historical Babi Yar Memorial, walking along pathways to the towering Motherland Statue, and eventually ending up at a bus plaza in the afternoon, looking for transportation to an outdoor architectural museum I'd read about.

Outdoor wooden architectural museum, near Kiev, Ukraine

The bus complex was large. Buses departed to outlying districts and other regions. I figured it was a long shot that a bus even went to the museum. I was tired. I studied the crowd, the Cyrillic signs, looking for a point of recognition, somebody to ask which bus to take. There were probably more than five hundred people in the plaza and dozens and dozens of buses, coming and going.

Across the plaza, I spotted a young couple, nicely dressed, who were standing by themselves, apparently waiting for something. They seemed approachable, so I walked over to them and asked if any buses went to the Outdoor Museum of Wooden Architecture, bumbling my pronunciation in the attempt.

They looked at me, absolutely surprised—not just because it was clear I was a foreigner but because they were waiting for the same bus to the same park. I was happily stunned and relieved.

Valentina invited me to accompany them and insisted on buying my ticket. The historical park was about twenty miles outside the city. We launched into a spirited conversation in Russian, trying to map out how this serendipitous moment had occurred. Anatoly smiled and engaged my limited command of Russian with a staccato of questions and humor. He would look at me directly at times, then his gaze seemed to wander from behind his smoke-tinted glasses, but he was warm and personable. I didn't know until we were well out into the countryside that Anatoly was blind.

I spent the day with them, walking along paths that wound through forests and hills where more than two hundred wooden buildings stood, all resurrected from past centuries. Anatoly asked that I call him Tolik, a more diminutive, personal name, and his wife, Valya.

Later that evening, sitting around their kitchen table, Tolik's fingers raced over the keys of his silver and black accordion. A wide smile played across his face, his head rolling easily, accenting every note, his right foot keeping rhythm. Everyone in the small apartment rode the crest of his melodic passages, listening to Georgian, Russian, Ukrainian, and Romani folk songs. Tolik's soulful rendition of *Midnight In Moscow* left me feeling pensive.

The evening reminded me of parties at home—friends gathered around a big table, simple food, a few bottles of wine, and music. A succession of dinner parties with old friends had spawned the band I had played in for the last ten years. A couple of the guests in Tolik's band had known each other since school days.

"It is best when bands and friends can be together over many years," he said.

Tolik had not been blind all his life. When he was twenty years old, he been studying to be a painter, like his father, but he lost his sight abruptly one night in an auto accident, when he plunged through a windshield. Five operations and fifteen years later, he still lived without eyesight but retained a great reservoir of humor.

"*Zhon! Zhon!*" he said, sitting at the table that night, pushing a plate of chicken sandwiches toward me. "More sandwiches? Ha, ha. Tomorrow you will have feathers—puck, puck, puck..."

"*Zhon!* Don't drink too much wine." His animation stirred laughter among friends. "*Boool, boool, boool, potom, xryou, xryou, xryou.*" Glug, glug, glug, then, oink, oink, oink.

"*Eta shootka.*" That's a joke, he'd say, after making any comical sound effects and comments.

I kept forgetting that he was blind and gestured with my hands to aid my conversation. Hand signals comprised an integral part of my Russian language ability.

I gave Tolik a cassette of our band. He put the tape in his player and turned up the stereo. He sat back, inclining his head toward the ceiling, and listened closely, refraining from conversation, absorbing the unfamiliar rhythms and vocals: Yankee rock, fused with reggae and African styles. He was enjoying the moment.

After listening to a couple songs, Tolik reached out and put his hand on my shoulder and said, "*Zhon*, this is great music. Tomorrow we'll take you to our concert hall, where we play music."

I was thrilled at his sincerity and the invitation to visit their music hall the next day. For the first time on the trip, I felt that the possibility that a joint music project was a real possibility and not just a farfetched idea that I'd dreamed up in a small town at the edge of the Pacific Ocean.

Valya looked at my photographs of friends and postcards of Northern California beaches, forests, and a volcano. I felt bad that Tolik couldn't see them, though he was just as interested as everyone else. He listened to Valya intricately describe the details of each picture, his imagination painting the scenes until he, too, could see the image.

Earlier that evening, Tolik had asked if I wanted to go for a walk and watch the sunset. Valya had gone to the grocery store to get some things for dinner, and he wanted to show me a few sights.

Guitarists from Tolik's band on stage at the blind institute

The front door to their apartment building opened onto a large asphalt and grass courtyard where a few cars were parked and a dozen children played. Two grandmothers sat on a bench and watched the children. Large chestnut trees lined both sides of the quiet, dead-end street in front of the building.

"Here comes the bus," I said, as we waited on a busy street corner several blocks away.

"That is the wrong bus," Tolik answered. He spoke only Russian. His voice resonated in a deep baritone.

"*Kak tee znaesh?*" How do you know?

"It sounds different." The first two buses ran on diesel. When the hum of an electric bus came, Tolik brushed my elbow. "This is our bus."

We rode the trolley bus toward the city center, winding through neighborhoods on wide boulevards. The ride cost about a nickel. Tolik talked the whole time.

"There is a park over there." He stared straight ahead but pointed out the other side of the window. "And there is a theater across the street. This is the district where I grew up. As a small boy, I played in that park."

The bus stopped more than a dozen times. Tolik kept talking and would occasionally reach out to find my arm. I wondered how he could possibly keep track of where we were.

"Here, we get off," he said abruptly.

"Where are we?" I asked.

"Near the river."

Tolik held my elbow as we walked quickly along the sidewalk. I'd known few people who walked as fast as I did.

"I like to walk fast," Tolik said, "This is my exercise, it's good for health."

Whenever we came to a curb, he always knew whether to step up or down and which way to turn at each corner, although sometimes he asked the name of the street. While walking back toward their home in the dark, beneath the chestnut trees on his street, I stumbled over a small steel pipe that was fixed across the sidewalk. But Tolik didn't stumble. He knew the pipe was there. He held my arm to steady me.

"Sorry," he said, chuckling, and clutching my arm, "I should have told you."

"Tolik," I joked, "you are my eyes."

The next day, I met Tolik and Valya at their apartment. We were joined by Tolik's sister, Sveta, and her boyfriend, Pasha, who was a musician and a Soviet soldier in the K9 corps. As we walked down the street together to the place Tolik's band played, we engaged in a rolling conversation full of humor and exclamations. Sveta, who had an infectious, deep laugh, was as energetic as her older brother.

"This is our hall," Tolik said as we approached a modest, three-story brick building in a residential neighborhood on a tree-lined street.

I soon learned that it was an institute for the blind, not just a music hall.

"Most the people here are blind," Tolik said.

We entered a large room where about forty people sat at technology benches, assembling electrical circuits. He led me over to one of the benches, where a young man was working and introduced me.

"This is Igor," he said. "He's the lead singer and songwriter in our band."

Igor at the blind institute, Jon and Tolik on the Dneiper River in Kiev

Igor turned with a wide smile and reached out to shake my hand, greeting me warmly in Russian. We spoke for a few minutes. Then he went back to his work.

Tolik led me through the building, introduced me to the director, took me through a couple more work areas and then to a *stolovaya*, where he said all the meals were free for the workers at the institute.

We stopped by a small clinic inside the building on the second floor, where people received free medical and dental care. We continued on to a culture hall on the main floor, which contained a stage and theater. That's where Tolik spent his time.

An enormous image of Lenin hung behind the stage as a backdrop, and the stage itself was equipped with an array of Soviet electric amplifiers and instruments and a PA system. Several of Tolik's musician friends from the institute were on the stage. A few had normal eyesight and worked in the supply and operations of the building.

Tolik switched on an electric keyboard, someone else flicked on the guitar amps, and the band launched into a practice session for an upcoming music event. I was carried away by the whole environment: the dynamics of the institute, hearing songs from Soviet popular culture, watching the interplay and the band stops, observing the exchange of dialogue to correct some arrangement and then back into the song. It was a familiar ritual.

Later in the afternoon, after the rehearsal session, I sat and played one of the electric guitars, with Tolik on keyboards. I introduced one of my songs, "Journey to the Red Planet." Igor, who I'd met earlier at his work bench, came into the hall and listened intently. We talked about the song. Tolik and Igor said my Russian translation "needed work" to be a real song. They were being polite.

Tolik and I hummed along on the melody and words. He and Igor asked me to leave my cassette copy of the song for them to work with, and Igor said he would develop a better translation. I was beyond thrilled to be there with two musicians from the USSR who had embraced and shared my imagination. The musical collaboration I had sought had finally taken root in a small theater in downtown Kiev.

Later that evening I came back to Tolik and Valya's apartment for another dinner. Sveta and Pasha were there, as were a few friends from the institute. After dinner, I took out my melodica, a small wind instrument with a double octave keyboard. I'd carried it with me the entire trip. Tolik became absorbed in a sound that was new to him. When I handed him the small, compact instrument, he ran his fingertips gently over every surface, feeling its shape, then put it to his lips and played as if he'd owned one for years.

One of Tolik's friends, a poet and a guitarist in his band, picked up a guitar and, with Tolik, wrote and sang a simple verse about our chance meeting.

> *"We all remain in expectation*
> *In this wonderful September evening*
> *We'll meet again, Zhon, our dearest one*
> *And we'll sing all together."*

Before I left their apartment that night, I gave the melodica to Tolik. He was astonished and grateful, and he and Valya both hugged me.

"We want you to have something Russian," Valya said. "For your home in America."

"Our Russian samovar," Tolik pointed toward an ornate electric urn, with a spigot and curved handles. "This is our gift. When you make tea, you will remember us, and this evening."

Tolik took the samovar off their shelf and presented it to me. Beneath my appreciative gestures and words, I wondered how I would ever be able to carry the thing halfway around the world without smashing it. The tea-making device was as bulky for traveling as a large crock pot, but delicate. I wasn't accustomed to carrying large appliances on my travels. In an instant, Valya boiled water in the samovar to prove that it worked, then disappeared out of the room, and returned with it packed snugly in its factory shipping container with a convenient rope handle lashed around the box. Now it was twice as big.

When I left their home, everyone accompanied me down the street toward the subway station. The guitarist in Tolik's band carried the box. We walked in the warm night air and waited for a bus on the corner. I didn't want to leave this haven of newfound friends, humor, and music. But I was locked into my travel plan. Tomorrow afternoon, I would be on the train back to Moscow.

Tolik insisted that they would all see me off on the train the next day—he, Valya, Sveta, and Pasha. It seemed a grand idea to extend our revelry through to the Kiev train station.

They met me at the hotel, and we took the bus to the station. We arrived an hour before the train's departure. Already in a great mood, we still had celebrating to do. Tolik pulled a bottle of vodka out of his satchel and said, "Let's drink to our time together!"

"Yes!"

We stood in a group of five and passed the bottle around, taking sips and bantering away. It was impossible not to be laughing, with Tolik and Sveta always charging the conversations through their energetic outbursts. I told an American joke in Russian that had everybody laughing. Pasha handed me a photograph of him and his K9 German Shepherd at a training ground as a memory. I had a

German Shepherd at home, and he and I had talked about our dogs. Valya had brought some Russian rye bread to have with the vodka shots.

Pasha and his K9 guard dog

It was one of those golden moments, when time is suspended and you are in the moment. The laughter was rooted deep in my chest. After about an hour, we suddenly remembered the train. I think it was Valya who came to her senses first. "The train!" she blurted. I looked at my watch with a sudden sinking feeling.

Everybody grabbed my luggage, and we started to run. We weren't even near the departure track. We had consumed the bottle of vodka in a corner of the main rail hall. There were probably six different departure tracks outside the station. Sveta and Pasha led the way on the run to the platform. We were a sorry group at that point, moving from revelry to panic in ten seconds flat.

The departure platform was the most distant from the hall. We ran as a group, Tolik holding onto Valya's arm. When we arrived out of breath, the train was nowhere in sight. It was gone. The reality of its departure sobered us up fast, but as we started looking around the situation became hilarious. We had arrived at the station a full hour early. Everything under control. Then, the vodka, laughter, and chaos.

In the end, I just took a later train to Moscow and got into the city in the late night, just hours before my next rail ticket was scheduled to depart to Belarus and Berlin. There would be little sleep that night, but the memories of the days in Kiev were riveted into my life.

Crossing Belarus

"Thirty minutes to the border. Passports prepared, please."

I sat up quickly. Thirty minutes to the border! The Soviet border. My pulse quickened. After two months of constant traveling within the borders of the Soviet Union, I was about to cross into Poland on my way to East Berlin. I'd boarded the train in Moscow the previous day to continue my rail journey across Russia and into Belarus.

Nina and her daughter were just waking in their bunks across from me. They greeted the morning lazily. I stepped out of the cabin and paced the corridor while they dressed in privacy.

Belarus countryside flashed by. I'd read Western travel accounts and heard stories of grueling luggage searches, rolls of film crudely developed on the spot, and written material confiscated. I'd copied the addresses of people I had met onto a small piece of paper, which I folded many times and placed in my shirt pocket.

I hurried to the car bathroom and tore up the original addresses, flushing them a few pieces at a time over at least two miles of track in case a special Soviet patrol searched for discarded information near the border. I checked my watch. Fifteen minutes to the border. I returned to my bunk and leafed through my journals—two months of travel notes.

The sound of footsteps in the corridor brought an image of armed guards. Soviet interrogation. Another knock on the door.

"Ten minutes to the border." The conductor slid the door open. "Passport?" I held up my American passport. He smiled. "Very good." He moved on to the next cabin and left our door open.

I looked over at my cabinmates. Their maroon Soviet passports lay on their laps. Erina's cheek rested against her mother's shoulder.

Era was seventeen, and her mother, Nina, was in her fifties. They were traveling to East Berlin to visit relatives. We had left Moscow the previous morning. Era had never traveled before and was fascinated by everything.

The two were a contrast of generations. Both were soft spoken, but Nina had the radiant glow of an older person very proud in her age and self-assured. Her eyes moved slowly and never darted away from contact. She wore no makeup, and she had several gold teeth. Era was pure teenager. She laughed a lot and dressed in a modern style. But her eyes were steady, like her mother's.

The train rolled into the Soviet border city of Brest. We bumped to a stop at the customs depot. Several border guards entered each car. Moments later, I heard the boots coming.

A young officer with a pleasant manner and no gun asked for our papers. He took mine first. "*Americanetz?*" he mused out loud. "*Odeen?*" One?

"*Da. Ya pootashestvavayou byez groop.*" Yes, I am traveling without a group.

He complimented me on my Russian language. It was getting better after two months in the USSR. He stepped out into the corridor with my passport and papers. I could hear his voice. "*Americanetz,*" he told the other guards. A guard with a face resembling Alfred E. Newman poked his head in the door for a look.

An officer of higher rank entered and raised his eyebrows while reading the list of cities and towns I'd visited from my visa. He grinned and asked me if I'd enjoyed my travels. His friendliness surprised me.

"*Da,*" I answered. "It is very interesting to be an American traveling in your country."

"Were the people good to you?"

"I met a lot of nice people."

The answer pleased him. He asked me a few more questions, prompted by his own curiosity, and then asked to see my luggage. I showed him the three pieces—the boxed samovar, a small, soft-sided suitcase, and my shoulder bag full of music tapes, journals, and rolls of film. I cut the twine and pried into my big box.

The officer turned his attention to Era and her mother. He asked Nina to step off the train after she showed a thick wad of rubles wrapped in a Soviet newspaper.

When she left the cabin, the officer sifted through my box without disturbing the tight packing job. Samovar, Georgian tea, books, records, wooden Ukrainian boxes. I opened the soft suitcase for his review. He fluffed through my clothes with his index finger.

"*Fsyo normalnaya.*" All was normal. He told me to stay with the train and that he would meet me in one hour to exchange my Soviet rubles for American dollars. Then he left.

I sat dumbfounded. That was it? The Soviet border? What about my other bag? The one with photos, tapes, journals, and camera? What about my mother's maiden name? Who won the world series in 1955? I felt ridiculous for flushing the addresses across Belarus.

The train jerked, then slowly rolled forward onto a siding, where a platoon of workers descended on the line of rail cars.

The Soviet pit crew worked quickly. In ten minutes, the entire train was hoisted six to eight feet off the ground by a series of enormous hydraulic jacks. All the Soviet wide-gauge wheel carriages were pulled away by hydraulic cables and replaced by the narrower, standard-gauge carriages that all the other European countries used. An ingenious system designed by one of the Russian tsars so invading countries couldn't run their trains on Russian rails.

I walked with Era through a greasy shop and out a big open door that led to a yard of rusting locomotive parts. The sky was gray. It was much cooler now. If there was any interrogation at the border, it came from Era's curiosity about life in America.

Half an hour later, the train lumbered back to the customs checkpoint with the new wheelsets beneath the carriages. The young officer guided me to a money exchange office and pointed toward a passage with a tiny glass window. A hand reached out the small opening, holding my passport and American dollars.

I was surprised to see American currency at a railroad facility on the border. But there they were, several crisp American twenty-dollar bills, with a few fives and tens. The exchange was all based on the Soviet currency system, where one ruble was the equivalent of one American dollar. I'd cashed in about 140 rubles. Outside the USSR, the Soviet ruble was almost worthless.

We rolled out of Brest Station with Soviet customs behind us. Just west of the city, I saw several Soviet border guards posted at a bridge over a small river. Guards on the other side of the bridge wore Polish military uniforms.

The small river reminded me of the creek on my grandparents' farm in the Sacramento Valley, where we used to catch bullfrogs and carp. It seemed a rather insignificant boundary. After traversing more than six thousand miles across the largest country in the world, this little creek signified the beginning of Polish territory. By contrast, America's western border was divided by a five-thousand-mile-wide ocean.

Polish customs were brief. The clouds had darkened, and rain began to fall. Our cabin took on a festive air. We were over the border. To celebrate, Era's mother pulled out the huge bag of food for a brunch. The cabin became a traveling buffet as she unloaded the satchel.

I'll call it motherly aggression—that woman attacked me with food. The previous evening, she'd shoved food at me until I was stuffed. Now it was starting all over again.

Era's mother kept saying, "*Koosheet, koosheet.*" Eat, eat.

I am, I am.

"And you are so skinny. There is much food. Have another of these."

Era giggled and tried to rescue me. "Mama, mama." She reached out and tried to intercept her mother's outstretched arm, which shook grapes and sandwiches at me.

I stepped out into the corridor to have a look out the north side of the train. The conductor asked how things were going with Nina and Era. He noticed how they'd taken me under their wing for the journey, buying all the tea and supplying all the meals. I blew my cheeks up and gestured a huge stomach. He enjoyed that.

"So you've traveled many places in Soviet Union?" he asked. "*Xarasho.*" Good. Since the moment I'd boarded the train in Moscow, the young conductor had made me feel like a special guest. He'd just returned from a month-long vacation and said it was difficult to get back to work.

We crossed into East Germany after dark. Era and her mother stared quietly out the window. They were holding hands and leaning against each other's shoulders.

Nina reached for the food bag again. "One more piece of bread," she urged. "This time, we must eat everything." I shrank at the thought of "everything."

The two were curious about food in California. Was it different? I tried to explain an avocado: pear-shaped, with soft green and yellow meat inside, and a seed the size of a plum; looks like a vegetable, grows on a tree, spreads like butter, and has the skin of an alligator. Next, I tried artichokes. Nina wrinkled her face and said something. I checked my dictionary. She didn't like thistles.

She wondered if there were any mushrooms where I lived. I said there were hundreds. She smiled. "Are forests and mushrooms in California like Russian forests and mushrooms?" she asked.

I told Nina some California mushrooms were exquisite for meals, some could send you on a hallucinogenic trip, and others might kill you. She nodded.

Down the corridor, a group of Russian tourists had been tipping a few and singing traditional songs, conveying a melancholy mood through the corridor into our cabin.

As the train drew near the East Berlin Station, I found the young conductor, thanked him, and gave him a postcard of a giant redwood tree, with a personal note written on the back in my best Russian handwriting. After reading the card, he shook my hand for a long time, struggling to say the right words, wanting to make sure I understood how happy he was to meet me. To meet someone from America.

"*Menye tozhe.*" Me too.

I went back to the cabin to sit with Era and Nina. Era helped me tie up my cardboard box with a better handle. I gave her ten postcards from California and a pocketful of international coins. We talked until the train bumped to a halt at the East Berlin railway station.

"Please, come to visit us in Siberia, in Novosibirsk." They gave me their address and best wishes as we picked up our bags.

The conductor waited in the corridor. He carried my heavy box through the narrow passage. We stood for a moment together on the platform, and he fumbled for something in his pocket.

"Here, take this," he urged. "My gift to you." He pressed a metallic object into my hand. The brass badge of the Soviet Railways, his official recognition.

I turned and looked back through the deserted railway station. Era, Nina, and the conductor stood together and waved one last farewell to me. It was almost midnight when I stepped into the streets of East Berlin. The specter of the Berlin Wall crept up on me from the darkness. But I felt optimistic. I had the railway badge in my pocket.

Yuri, from Kamchatka

Our boat lifted sharply on a big swell, then rolled far to the port side. At the top of the next sea, I focused my binoculars on a Soviet ship that lay five miles off the Northern California coast, near the entrance to Humboldt Bay. The *Ratmonova* drifted in slow motion over moderate swells. Two red smokestacks jutted from the vessel's white superstructure, both stacks emblazoned with a yellow hammer and sickle.

My stomach hollowed as our boat dropped fifteen feet off another wave. The ocean swells were steep and close together on the bar. Jim Walters stood at the wheel of his fifty-foot sport fishing party boat, the *Sail Fish*. He'd been hired to transfer Yuri, a young Soviet fisherman, to his ship. Yuri had just spent a week being treated at a local hospital, recovering from emergency surgery.

Yuri motioned to my stomach with a spinning motion. "*Chushvavaesh xarasho?*" he asked, wondering if the rolling seas upset my equilibrium. I shook my head and said, "*Fsyo normalnaya.*" All was normal. He grinned.

The boat lurched down again. Yuri grabbed the corner of a bench to steady himself, then turned his gaze seaward. Eight days had passed since he'd seen his Soviet crewmates.

The voice of an American observer aboard the *Ratmonova* boomed in over the radio.

"That's Phillip," Yuri said, pointing toward the radio. Jim reached for the radio mike and answered the *Ratmonova*'s call. The *Ratmonova*'s captain would launch one of their lifeboats to rendezvous with the *Sail Fish*.

Jim hung up the radio mike and reached into a box under the instrument console and came up with some printed brochures. "Here's some propaganda," he laughed, handing Yuri some advertisements for his party boat business.

"Thank you ... thank you very much." Yuri stammered one of the few English expressions he knew. Our eyes met comfortably. Four days before, we had been total strangers.

The first day I met Yuri, he was asleep in his hospital bed. A ward nurse woke him from his nap. "Yuri, you have a visitor." He scrambled up to a sitting position, wiping his eyes and brushing back his sandy brown hair.

"*Zdrastvweetye*." Hello.

Yuri looked half awake, but he quickly motioned to a chair. "*Sideetsya pozhalsta*." He asked me to please sit down. A stack of sports magazines covered the nightstand. I noticed vases of fresh flowers at his bedside. We introduced ourselves. His hand felt strong and rough from handling rigging in the salt air.

I told him I'd read in the newspaper about his arrival and wanted to see how he was feeling and to practice my Russian conversation.

Yuri looked surprisingly energetic. He'd had surgery only three days before but dismissed the appendectomy as "*choot, choot,*" a little nothing.

I handed Yuri a copy of Ivan Turgenev's play *A Month in the Country*, printed in Russian. He thanked me, thumbed through it for a moment, then set it aside in favor of our conversation. I told him of my trip across the Soviet Union within the last year. He wanted to know what I thought about his country. We talked for about an hour in Russian that first day. He accommodated my vocabulary by speaking more slowly and choosing simpler expressions. Mostly he talked about his family and the sea.

Yuri was twenty-five years old. He and his wife and daughter lived in Petropavlovsk Kamchatka, on the Kamchatka Peninsula, in the Soviet Far East. But he'd grown up in a Ukrainian town on the Sea of Azov, where his parents and grandparents still lived.

He'd been at sea for six months, fishing from the coast of North America to the South Pacific Islands. He hadn't seen his family in the past half year, but he and his wife wrote letters and sent messages to each other on the ship's wireless. Yuri and Irina had been married for a couple of years and had a baby daughter. Little Natasha would be one year in just eight days.

Yuri seemed relaxed and in good spirits despite being plucked off his Soviet ship by the United States Coast Guard with five minutes' notice and dropped into an American hospital for an emergency appendectomy. Nurses hurried in and out on their rounds. Yuri would smile when they tried to talk to him in English. Some of them spoke louder as if he had a hearing problem.

I returned to the hospital the following morning and asked Yuri if he wanted to visit a "redwood factory." He didn't know what the doctor would say. I told him everything had been cleared, the doctor said he needed exercise. Yuri climbed out of bed.

"Please, a moment to prepare."

An hour later, we stood in the Pacific Lumber Company's giant Scotia Mill peering through thick glass windows at an enormous hydraulic debarking machine.

The entire building shook when the big redwood timbers were bounced around by a mechanical, clawed monster. It was quite a change from Yuri's hospital room. We walked along the overhead catwalks, stopping periodically to observe various milling stations. Yuri told me the Russian terms for the machines we saw.

He leaned over the railing and watched a multi-ton redwood log roll aboard the band saw's diesel log carriage. The carriage shook and surged back and forth rapidly, its mechanical reverberations pulsing through the mill. The band saw shrieked as it ripped six-inch-thick slabs of lumber the length of the log.

"*Tak bweestra!*" Yuri shouted. So fast! We stopped to observe a laser-guided edger saw. The re-saw building occupied floor space equal to a dozen football fields. Yuri was amazed by the size of the mill.

"Near Petropavlovsk we have sawmills." Yuri yelled above the din of machinery. "But not this big!"

Yuri lived in the largest country in the world, where accomplishments were often measured by magnitude. The Soviet Union produced more oil and cement than any country; it boasted the largest merchant fleet and the biggest airline. Yuri was impressed. The Pacific Lumber Company was the largest redwood mill in the world.

We drove south to Rockefeller Forest, in the Humboldt Redwoods State Park, where we parked the car and followed a footpath into a grove of giant redwoods. Most of the trees towered more than three hundred feet. Yuri paused for a moment to look up at them. Patches of sunlight filtered down onto the fern-covered forest floor. "The quiet—it is beautiful." Yuri looked all around. "I wish Irina could see where I am standing."

Yuri lifted the thin gold chain that he wore around his neck. A gold zodiac sign hung from it. Scorpio. "This is Irina's zodiac sign. She wears my zodiac. So we are always with each other."

He tucked the zodiac back into his collar and pulled a pack of Russian cigarettes from his pocket, looking over his shoulder as though hiding from someone.

"Irina would be angry if she knew I smoked right now. She doesn't like it."

Yuri kept pausing to look up at the great trees. Children's laughter carried up from the nearby Eel River. We stopped.

"Ah ... *deity*," Yuri said the Russian word for children. We watched about a dozen children and their families picnicking around a swimming hole.

I offered Yuri some blackberries, plums and small tomatoes I had purchased from a roadside produce stand along the highway.

"We must go," I glanced at my watch. "I have to meet other people today." I didn't tell Yuri that I would be late. He would have felt badly. He'd already asked me if I was sure I had enough time to show him around.

"I will always remember these trees," he said, gazing one last time at the tallest trees in the world.

Over the next two days, Yuri and I toured the far corners of Humboldt County, taking in an outdoor reggae music concert, a museum of Native American basket weavings, a steam-powered logging exhibition, ocean beaches, and the commercial fishing fleet.

Taking Yuri to Reggae on the River was a bit of a stretch. Even a lot of Americans wouldn't feel comfortable at that event. We spent the day together at the concert. It was staged on a knoll in the countryside, at the edge of the Eel River, in southern Humboldt County, about sixty miles south of the hospital where Yuri was being treated.

We sat under the hot sun and listened to the rhythmic pulse of a band from Kingston, Jamaica. I had lunch for us in a small cooler. Mid-afternoon, I handed Yuri a tuna sandwich and a bottle of mineral water from the cooler while we listened to the bands.

Yuri took a few bites of the sandwich and raised one eyebrow trying to figure out what he was eating. "*Shto eta?*" he asked, pointing at his sandwich. I'd mixed in sweet relish and mayonnaise, so it didn't taste fishy. I gave him too much information, saying this fish swims with dolphins.

"You know about dolphins?" I abstractly linked the two in my mind since they swim together and feed on similar bait. Yuri heard the word dolphin, and his eyes nearly popped out.

"No, no!" I quickly interrupted. "The sandwich isn't dolphin. *Nyet* dolphin." Yuri looked relieved.

"*Tunyetz,*" I said.

"Ah, *tunyetz!*"

He told about a time when the *Ratmonova* was anchored near Tahiti and a school of dolphins played at the side of the ship with a soccer ball that one of the crew had thrown to them.

Each time we met someone that day, people wished Yuri safe travels and peace between our countries, the mirror image of my passage through the USSR.

He looked happy and relaxed at the concert. He liked the music, especially the more rock-oriented American bands. The huge sound system flooded the valley with music.

"*Xaroshaya shoom.*" I said, confidently. Yuri started laughing.

"*Nyet shoom. Xaroshaya zvuke,*" he corrected, using his hands and ears to indicate something more pleasant. I'd just said it was great noise, instead of great sound.

We walked down to the Eel River a few times and waded out into the shallow water to get relief from the ninety-degree heat.

Near the end of the day, a friend brought her eleven-month-old baby girl to meet Yuri. Alyssum's first birthday would be in ten days, within two days of Yuri's daughter's birthday. I told him the little blue-eyed wonder who held his outstretched finger in her tiny grip was the same age as Natasha. For several minutes, Yuri gazed at her. I'm sure he imagined how his daughter had grown while he'd been at sea for the last half year. Yuri cooed little Russian words to Alyssum and pressed his fingers against her chubby arms and cheeks.

"*Ya lyoublyou deity.*" I love children, he said.

The next day, we went down to the Humboldt Bay waterfront, where my father's commercial fishing boat was moored. Both my parents were aboard to meet Yuri.

"This boat would probably fit in the hold of your ship," my father said as he welcomed Yuri aboard. My translation lost the essence of the joke, giving Yuri the idea that my father wanted to drop his boat down the hold of the *Ratmonova*.

We stepped into the pilothouse, and Yuri looked around, approving of the electronics.

"*Radar, da?*" Yuri pointed at the screen. A universal word.

My mother had never met anyone from the Soviet Union before. She'd grown up in American farm country and was interested that Yuri's grandparents raised bees, vegetables, and fruit on their small farm in Ukraine.

Yuri and my father stood together on the rear deck, near the fish hold, smoking cigarettes, two sailors who loved the sea. When my dad was Yuri's age, he worked as a seaman in the merchant marine. One winter in Vladivostok, Russian sailors toting vodka bottles took him on a wild sleigh ride down a waterfront street. I waded into that translation and was quickly over my head in sea stories. Yuri and my father wanted to tell each other about ships colliding, towboats, icebergs, and waterfront brawls.

On Yuri's last day ashore, we drove north to Trinidad.

"This is a good highway," Yuri observed, as we buzzed along 101. We passed a purple 1956 Cadillac that had been chopped, channeled, and customized into a funky pickup truck with chrome "laker pipes" and wide wheels. Yuri eyed it curiously.

"What kind is that car?"

"Cadillac." I knew this would be difficult. I tried to explain the American fascination with automobiles. "Some people sculpt their cars."

"Yes? Automobile artists?" Yuri raised his eyebrows, bewildered. It was impossible to explain some things.

"I have a television in my Zhiguli!" Yuri said.

"Say that again?"

"There is TV in my car."

"It's dangerous to watch TV and drive, no?" I reached to the dashboard of my car and pretended to change channels and not watch the road.

"No. Not to drive with TV. Only if the car is stopped." Yuri laughed.

He had a four-inch-diagonal TV that plugged into a cigarette lighter. He kept it in the glove compartment and watched it if he had to wait somewhere or if a winter storm hit and he had to pull off the road.

In Trinidad, we walked out onto the headland. A six-foot-wide rocky ledge on the northwest bluffs proved to be a good vantage point. Yuri liked being near the sea again. This was the first time he'd been close to the ocean since coming ashore the previous week.

"Few Russians have ever stood on this rock." I told him that the peg-legged sea captain Ivan Kuzkov had been here in the early 1800s, when the Russians settled on the north coast of California farther south, at Fort Ross.

We sat on the ledge and listened. Sea lions barked like a pack of hounds, white water foamed over Trinidad's reef, seagulls uttered shrill cries, and the harbor buoys moaned and clanged.

"This reminds me of home." Yuri was watching the horizon. Somewhere beyond his sight was the *Ratmonova* and his shipmates. And way beyond that was his home and his family on the Kamchatka Peninsula.

He described a tradition of his home port. When a ship returned after being at sea, the crew would toss coins into the water around the three large rocks named Three Brothers to repay them for helping them return safely. I told Yuri that ninety kilometers to the north, beyond our sight, were three offshore rocks that protruded from the ocean called the Three Sisters.

I asked Yuri what his ship did at sea, and what kind of fish they caught. A lot of people in the coastal communities of Northern California thought the Russians were taking salmon. "*Losas, nyet.*" No salmon.

Yuri said that at home, near Kamchatka, they caught salmon, but that off the coast of the U.S. mainland, they only processed hake. None of the Soviet fleet even fished. They were strictly offshore buyers. All the hake were caught by U.S. trawlers and the nets transferred to the Soviets, who cleaned and iced the hake, paying the American fishermen for each net load. One of Yuri's jobs was to handle the rigging as the American nets were winched aboard. U.S. observers were stationed on each Russian ship.

"Tomorrow I will go." Yuri spoke with resolve.

"Have you heard yet?" I asked.

"No, but they promised me I would go on Monday."

"Soviet person?"

"Yes, from Seattle. He telephoned me."

"And what if they don't come for you tomorrow?" I asked.

"They will come," he answered, looking out at the vacant horizon.

I looked at my watch. My friend was expecting us for dinner. By the time we reached her house, the August sun was low in the western sky. A couple of puffy clouds navigated the horizon line. The house sat on a cliff about two hundred feet above the ocean. We could see thirty miles down the coast, almost to Cape Mendocino. It was like being aboard a ship. The grassy cliff extended out about forty feet, then dropped to the ocean. Yuri stood staring to the south and then to the north. "To live so close to sea is good."

His wife's parents had built a small dacha on the Kamchatka Coast, just outside Petropavlovsk. Their windows looked onto the Pacific Ocean from the east. Our sunset would be their sunrise.

We sat down at a table next to a large, open window. The sounds and smells of the seashore drifted in. Yuri was curious about the cost of housing in the U.S. He folded his hands and looked as if he were swallowing a horse pill as he contemplated the numbers.

"We pay $12.50 a month for our apartment," he said. That wasn't much considering that he made $800 a month, four times the average Soviet wage. But he had to be away from home for months at a time.

Toward sunset, we lit a fire in a rock-lined fire pit. We brought out a large cast iron skillet of potatoes, onions, and herbs and placed it on a grill over one corner of the fire. Over the flames, we could see the waves as the smoke drifted to the south.

Yuri looked interested in the food. He hadn't enjoyed some of the hospital meals. At one lunch, he'd sniffed suspiciously at a leaf of lettuce, taken a bite, and wrinkled his face. "Bad cabbage." He missed his Russian bread and thought the spongy, white hospital bread tasted like cotton.

"It's good to sit in front of a fire again," Yuri said, gazing into the coals. "I can watch fire all night. It's better than TV."

Yuri talked about the Srednyaya Mountains where he and Irina liked to hike. They would tent camp in the forest and cook over an open flame. In the winter, they would cross-country ski into the mountains and soak in natural hot pools near a volcano.

"Everything is simple then," Yuri said. "I've got a car and stereo, very interesting things, but people lived for many years without them. We can't live without fire."

We sat by the fire as the night sky unleashed diamonds. It didn't matter that Yuri was from Russia or that we were Americans. Sitting around a fire eating potatoes, people could just be themselves.

At 11:30 the next morning I called the hospital, and the ward nurse told me that Yuri's ship had arrived off the Humboldt coast. But he had no idea what was going on. I drove to the hospital to translate the news.

When I walked into Yuri's room, he was reading. I told him that in thirty minutes he would be leaving the hospital to meet his ship.

"Yes?" He was enthusiastic.

He quickly got up, showered, and dressed. A nurse brought a lunch tray for him. He poked through it, eating only half a sandwich and drinking a cup of tea. He seemed anxious. He made brief phone calls to thank two local Russian-speaking people who had also befriended him during his stay in Humboldt County.

At noon, the stevedore agent strode in. Through my father's waterfront connections, I'd arranged for Jim Walters and the *Sail Fish* to deliver Yuri back to his ship. The agent handed Yuri his passport and some other documents. Yuri signed a few more papers at the ward desk and said his goodbyes. We hurried down to the car and drove out to the south bay community of King Salmon. Jim Walters was aboard the *Sail Fish*, with the twin diesels warming up.

Once we were a few miles offshore, Yuri and I watched his ship appear on the northern horizon and advance swiftly toward us. The name, *Ratmonova*, stood out clearly in large, white Cyrillic letters against the black steel hull. Smoke billowed from the double stacks. White water boiled at its stern. The three-hundred-foot ship swung around to face northeasterly. It hardly rolled.

Jim cut back the *Sail Fish*'s throttle as we moved in on the leeward side of the giant fishing vessel. I could make out faces of crewmen that lined the rails. Four men scampered up a narrow ladder into the *Ratmonova*'s starboard lifeboat. Almost immediately, winches lowered the smaller vessel down the side of the ship into the water. The enclosed lifeboat bore an odd resemblance to a red fiberglass septic tank.

Yuri and I stepped down into the galley.

"Write me if you can," I said. "And good luck. You are a friend to me." My simplistic Russian always left me short of what I wanted to say. I handed him a cassette tape of our band's music. The title seemed tailored for the moment, "Sail Away." Yuri nodded his head and thanked me.

"You are a friend, too. I will always remember you." We shook hands one last time. "*Shastleevway.*"

Yuri turned quickly and stepped out onto the rear deck. The *Ratmonova*'s lifeboat came in alongside the *Sail Fish*. Both boats rolled in the seas, lifting ten to twelve feet then dropping. A salty, stubble-faced seaman smoking a cigar and wearing an orange hard hat maneuvered the lifeboat close.

"*Kak delo?*" One of the sailors yelled over the clatter of diesels and splashing waves to Yuri. How are things going?

"*Ochen xarasho,*" he yelled back. Really good.

A sailor emerged from the covered lifeboat with a sack of something. He walked over to the rail, steadied himself, and started swinging the sack in circles over his head and then let it fly toward our boat. Yuri caught it. He presented it to me. It was a bag of freshly baked Russian rye bread from the ship's galley. Yuri had somehow gotten word to the ship that we were impoverished when it came to bread. We all had a good laugh.

Yuri turned for a last glance goodbye, then stepped up onto the rail of the *Sail Fish*. Both boats rose on the top of another sea. The geographical separation of our two countries diminished to a four-foot gap of turbulent water. Yuri jumped the void. His mates caught him. I threw his travel bag through the forward hatch to a third seaman, who gave me thumbs up. The lifeboat veered away. And that was it.

Yuri had left America and was back aboard his ship. He waved from the open hatch a couple of times before they reached the *Ratmonova*.

Yuri and his shipmates made it safely aboard. I watched them climb down the narrow ladder to the ship's main deck and disappear through an open doorway.

Once again the radio blared.

"*Sail Fish*. This is *Ratmonova*. On behalf of the captain and the crew, we would like to thank you and the agent for all that has been done and the great care you have taken to assist our crewman."

Jim handed me the mike. "Go ahead, they want to talk to the agent."

I wasn't exactly the agent, but I took the gray plastic mike and pushed the broadcast button.

"Thank you, *Ratmonova*. I wish you safe travels at sea." I finished the broadcast in Russian, thinking that it might surprise the captain to hear his native language over the American marine radio. "We were all happy to meet Yuri. Now, his health is good. I hope that in the future, the Soviet Union and America will live together in peace. Thank you. May good fortune be with you. *Sail Fish*, out."

Jim turned east toward the Humboldt Bar and opened up the throttle on both diesels. Black smoke rose from the *Ratmonova*'s double stacks. The Soviet ship turned northwest, powering over the tops of the swells.

"This is the *Ratmonova*. The captain has a message for you."

"Viva, America! *Ratmonova*, out."

Seven Years Later...

I was standing on stage at Humboldt State University's Van Duzer Theater, in Arcata, California, with fifteen musicians from Moscow and Humboldt County lining the stage behind me. It was December 3, 1992.

The theater was filled with hundreds of people who had come to hear the Timezone Concerts—an international world beat production that had taken us almost ten years to produce. The stage was loaded with percussion instruments, kettle drums, two trap sets, electric guitars, a pedal steel, amplifiers, keyboards, traditional folk instruments, and rows of microphones. Video cameras and recording equipment were rolling.

The university's Center Arts director had taken a keen interest in Timezone after hearing the story of the project and had offered the university's support and facilities to help bring the event to a live audience. It would be a three-night concert series, with each night building in attendance. The live musical program was three hours long, filled with original songs and some traditional folk pieces.

Under the glare of stage lights, after a month of live rehearsals at the theater, I introduced the band and we kicked off the first of three, live Timezone Concerts.

Timezone onstage at Humboldt State University's Van Duzer Theater, December 3, 1992

After that first trip across Siberia and the USSR, I'd gone back to Kiev in 1987 to find Tolik and his friends and pursue the idea of playing music together. The idea of a musical bridge had never left me. They'd translated my first song—"Journey to the Red Planet"—into Russian and Hebrew and had been singing it in Kiev. But Chernobyl had erupted a year before, making it hard to set any solid plans because of the uncertainty caused by the accident. Tolik didn't write about Chernobyl in his letters, though, other than to say everybody was fine. I think he was being cautious about government censorship.

He also hadn't known exactly when I would return to Ukraine. He expected me, but only in a very general sense. I arrived in Kiev unannounced and walked to the neighborhood where he and Valya lived. They weren't home. In the years before cell phones, our correspondence was all by letters, which took weeks to arrive. It had been a long shot to try to make all this happen.

Later in the day, Tolik and Valya appeared, walking down the street, arm in arm. We had a joyous reunion that turned into dinners, music, and a big gathering of their friends.

We did an overnight camping trip up the Dneiper River, north of Kiev, toward Chernobyl, visited with Tolik's and Valya's families and recorded "Journey to the Red Planet" on a small, four-track recorder I'd brought with me into the Soviet Union on a ferry via Estonia.

In the end, it was the friendship, trust, and personal connections with Tolik and Valya and their circle of friends in Kiev that became the catalyst that launched the Timezone Project.

I went back to Kiev again in 1988. I traveled out to Lvov, taking in more of Ukraine. I attended the wedding of one of Tolik and Valya's friends and stayed at Valya's parents' home. These were personal, intimate visits.

Valya and Pasha along a river near Kiev

But I was also meeting new people in Moscow at the same time and was growing more committed to producing Timezone. One of the Sashas that Layla had introduced me to in 1984 in Moscow had been able to secure homestay visas for me so that hotels were no longer required.

Some of my Moscow connections were involved in the city's vibrant and experimental underground music scene. I had a dozen songs written to varying degrees of completion by 1989, looking for broader collaboration and more professional recording venues. Those opportunities opened up significantly in Moscow.

Several Moscow musicians from the underground scene immediately took an interest in Timezone. Through them, I met a well-known Russian folk musician and a phenomenal drummer from Dushanbe, Tajikistan. We bribed a government recording studio engineer to give us after-hours access to high-quality, 24-track recording gear and laid down the basic tracks to what would become the Timezone album, *Lost Nations*.

Then I flew recording reels back and forth between Humboldt County and Moscow, overdubbing Moscow musicians on California tracks and California musicians on Moscow tracks. The California recordings were engineered by Robby Jarvis at Humboldt Records, who I'd played music with for over 20 years.

I was in and out of Moscow numerous times between 1988 and 1991. I carried reel-to-reel tapes with me, and the border guards never objected. Russian overdubs were finished in a Moscow underground recording studio under the guidance of Pyotr Mamonov, one of Moscow's great avant-garde musicians.

We were riding the wave of a rapid cascade of events that had begun to unfold across Eastern Europe and the Soviet Union.

Mikhail Gorbachev was elected, Glasnost emerged; the Berlin Wall came down; I met an inspiring young journalist at a dinner party in Moscow, and a year later we were engaged at a private home on Lake Seliger, in the Volga Basin; Gorbachev was arrested the following morning; tanks and armored columns rolled into Moscow; Timezone recordings were paused; more than one hundred thousand people went to Freedom Square to stand against the military coup; Gorbachev was released; Oxana and I got married in Moscow, December 3, 1991; the Timezone recordings were completed in Moscow the week the Soviet Union collapsed; we flew back to California via Siberia and Alaska with the tape reels and did the final mix of the *Lost Nations* album at Russian Hill Recording Studios in San Francisco; and six months later, we staged the live concerts at Humboldt State University. The project had taken almost ten years and one hundred thousand miles of flights to complete.

That night on the stage at Van Duzer Theater, I felt completely overwhelmed by the magnitude of events coalescing around the concerts. After ten years—chasing a dream, imagining an event, persevering through hundreds of interactions with people on both sides of the world, through two languages, all the conversations, the bouts of self-doubt, the miles of travel on planes, ships, and trains, the obstacles, the musical interplays, getting married in the midst and celebrating our first anniversary that night on the stage—I was ready to let it all go and just play the music.

In the Timezone Concert, we'd collaborated to create more than fifteen original songs that would be played live, for the first time. At the end of the final night, to a standing ovation, I thanked the crowd, the university, and the musicians. I acknowledged that we would all be going our separate ways after that night but that the songs and the hope that this musical journey had kindled would live on in the memory of our music and having come together to create it.

Reference Notes

Listen to Timezone music:

Bandcamp.com has the original 10 songs from the 1992 *Lost Nations* album, plus Bill Laswell's Reconstruction & Mixtranslation from 2015, and a second Laswell remix from 2019.

timezone1.bandcamp.com/album/lost-nations

Apple iTunes Store has the 2015 *Lost Nations: Reconstruction & Mixtranslation by Bill Laswell*

music.apple.com/us/album/lost-nations-reconstruction-mixtranslation-by-bill/981714770

Photo Credits:

All photos by Jon Humboldt Gates, except the following:
Front Cover Photo – Siberian Village on the Angara – by Elenmay; iStockphoto
Back Cover Photo – Hydrofoil Ferry – commons.wikimedia.org
Back Cover Photo – Trans Siberia at Lake Baikal – by Maxim Petrichuk – Dreamstime.com
Page 20-21 – Train Photo – Trans Siberia – by Mircea Preda Struteanu – Dreamstime.com
Page 32 – Lake Baikal, high-speed hydrofoil – by Keyclub11 – Dreamstime
Page 52–53 – Soviet Film Billboard – Photo by Phil Greenberg
Page 59 – Jake – Photo by Erik, from Usolye-Sibirskoye
Page 74 (right) – Church of Ascension at Kolomenskoye – by Juliasha – Dreamstime
Page 142 – Pasha and his K9 – Pasha's personal collection
Page 164, 166–167 – Timezone on stage at Van Duzer Theater – Photo by Gary Davidson

Acknowledgements

The second edition, *It's Warm in Siberia*, has come about with the assistance and editorial guidance of Katie Sanborn, friend and editor for over 30 years, who has edited hundreds of my business-related stories as well as my last two books—*Firestorm* and *Before the Dolphins Guild*. Additionally, I have much appreciation for Renée Davis, who I've worked with also for over 20 years, for her design and layout of all my books, print and e-books, including this Second Edition, and two earlier titles that have been reissued.

In retrospect, I owe a great debt of gratitude to all who helped bring my original manuscript for *Soviet Passage* to life back in 1984, especially, to Teresa Porter—who embraced the story and helped bring the manuscript into book form through her Summer Run Publishing venture, in Eureka, California. And to Beverly Hanley, who provided artistic and editorial guidance that helped craft the narration of the original edition. Also, to Lis Skarrup of Denmark, for giving me the gift of the Russian language—the key that opened my travels—while teaching at our local university. She also was an inspiration in bringing this story to print and remains a lifelong friend.

And in memory of my parents, Irene and Humboldt Gates. Irene proofread the manuscript four times, with a tremendous eye for detail. Humboldt lit up my imagination with his stories of old Russian Alaska and sailing into Vladivostok in the 1930s when he was in the merchant marine.

A special appreciation to my original cast of readers from 1984, who pondered various stages of the manuscript and offered constructive critiques: Peter Chordas, Dina Bernadine, Raymond Donnell, Margot Genger, Joyce Hough, Fred Neighbor, and Steve Docktor.

To Tolik, Valya, Vova, Svyeta and Pasha of Kiev for their inspired gatherings and friendship that ignited an international music collaboration, as well as Yuri, from Petropavlovsk, Kamchatka, who came to Humboldt County by sea.

And lastly, but of greatest consequence, a recognition of life-changing decisions that my wife, Oxana, has contributed to the whole process over the years—

from our engagement at the headwaters of the Volga River, to the streets of Moscow during the 1991 USSR military coup, and ultimately, her will and courage, to leave her work, her friends, her family, and her homeland, to join me in exploring a future full of uncertainties, on the other side of the world.

About the Author

Jon Humboldt Gates is the author of five nonfiction books, including his most recent historical work: *Before the Dolphins Guild – A Story of Heroic Efforts to Save Two Navy Submarine Crews Trapped Under the Sea in 1915 and 1916* (2022).

Jon got his literary start recording and narrating oral history interviews with older people from his hometown region of Humboldt County, California in the 1970s and 1980s as well as chronicling his numerous solo journeys across North America and the USSR. His archives of oral history provided  the basis for his first two books: *Falk's Claim – The Life and Death of Redwood Lumber Town* (1983), nominated for The Forest History Award in 1984, and *Night Crossings – Maritime Stories of Rogue Waves at Night on California's Notorious Humboldt Bar* (1986). Both books are now in their seventh printings.

The author also wrote *Firestorm (2018) – A Personal Narrative from the Epicenter of the Tubbs Firestorm, One of the Most Destructive Wildfires in California History*.

During his 35-year career as a market journalist, Jon conducted thousands of personal interviews in supply chains around the world. He eventually became Director of Global Research for the international firm OTR Global, which he co-founded with friends in San Francisco in 1995.

Jon is a fifth-generation native of Northern California and the Pacific Northwest. His great-great-grandparents came West by wagon train in 1849, and his grandfather was a miner in the Klondike Gold Rush in 1900. He and his wife now live near the Columbia River in Oregon.

Other Works

Before the Dolphins Guild
A story of heroic efforts to save two Navy submarine crews
trapped under the sea in 1915 and 1916
Moonstone Publishing

Firestorm
A personal narrative: Vignettes from the epicenter of the 2017 Tubbs Fire –
one of the most destructive wildfire in California history
Moonstone Publishing

Falk's Claim
The Life and Death of a Redwood Lumber Town
Moonstone Publishing

Night Crossings
A half-century of maritime encounters with rogue waves in the night while
crossing California's notorious Humboldt Bar
Moonstone Publishing

Soviet Passage (1st Edition)
Travel stories and photography from a solo journey across Russia and Siberia in 1984
Summer Run Publishing

Lost Nations (CD)
The Timezone Band
Russian-American worldbeat music collaboration in 1991
Moonstone Publishing

Lost Nations (MP3)
The Timezone Band
Reconstruction and mixtranslation by Bill Laswell
M.O.D *Technologies, New York, NY*

www.ingramcontent.com/pod-product-compliance
Lightning Source LLC
Chambersburg PA
CBHW050416120526
44590CB00015B/1985